JUNE McKINNON

A Tapestry of Lives

Cape Women of the 17th Century

KWELA BOOKS

My grateful thanks to Annari van der Merwe for believing in me, to Henrietta Rose-Innes for her inspired editing, to all the librarians at the South African Library and the archivists at the South African Archives for their help over many long hours of research, to Phillida Brooke Symons for her ever-ready advice, and to Professor Robert Shell for his expertise and optimistic guidance.

Kwela Books acknowledges with gratitude
the financial support of this project by the Prince Claus Fund

as well as the National Arts Council of South Africa.

c/o Kwela Books
40 Heerengracht, Cape Town 8001;
P.O. Box 6525, Roggebaai 8012
kwela@kwela.com

Cover design by Alexander Kononov
Cover illustration: *T'Kaness* by S Daniell
Typography by Nazli Jacobs
Set in Minion
Printed and bound by Paarl Print, Oosterland Street, Paarl, South Africa

First edition, first printing 2004
ISBN 0-7957-0122-5

http://www.kwela.com

To my beloved late husband John,
the ultimate "feminist",
for his love and encouragement.

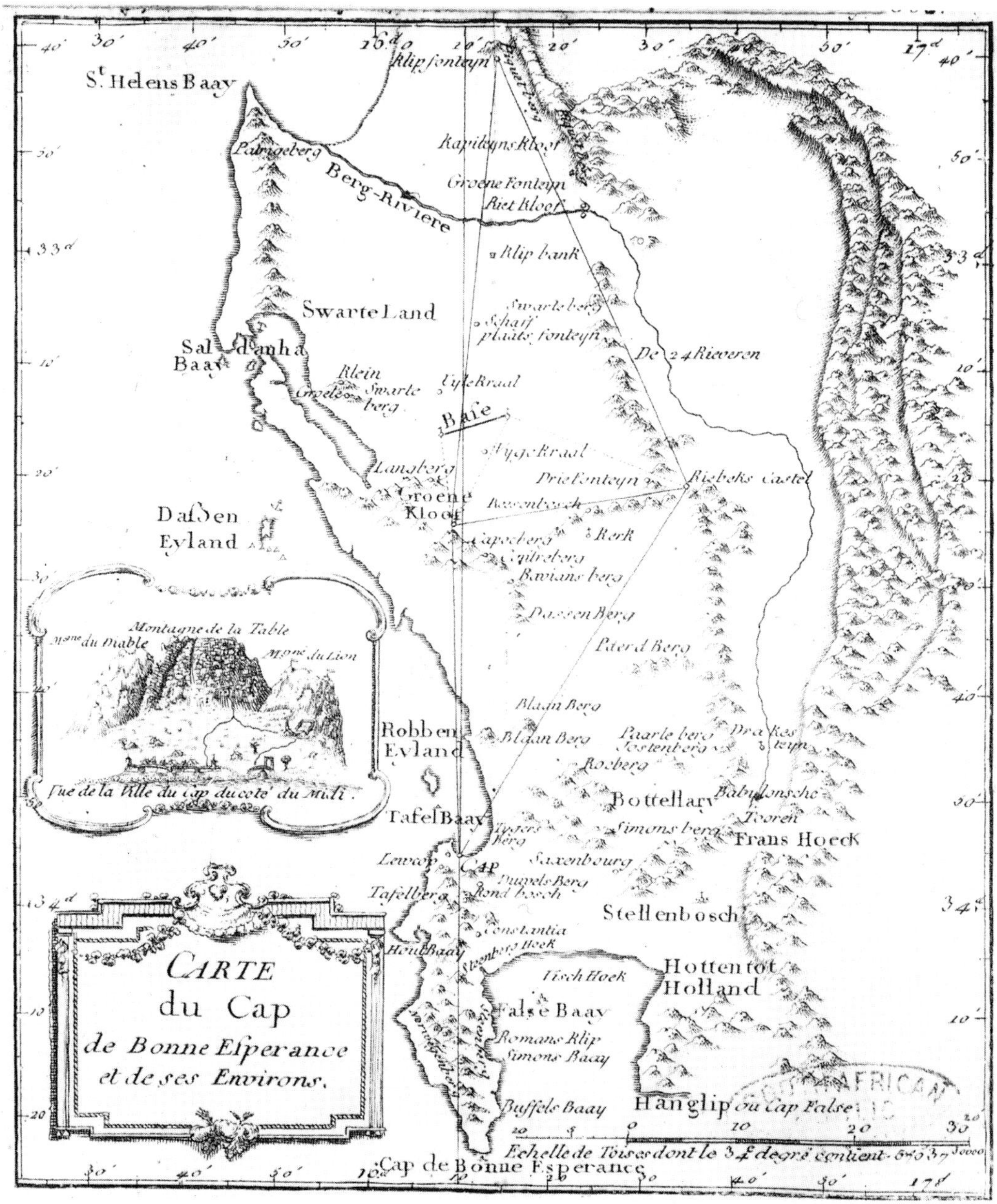

CARTE du Cap de Bonne Esperance et de ses Environs.

Montagne de la Table
Mgne du Diable
Mgne du Lion
Vue de la Ville du Cap du coté du Midi.

St. Helens Baay
Klip fonteyn
Kapiteyns Kloof
Groene Fonteyn
Riet Kloof
Berg-Riviere
Klip bank
Swarte Land
Swarte berg
Schaff plaats fonteyn
Sal danha Baay
De 24 Rieveren
Klein Swarte berg
Vyle Kraal
Base
Langberg
Groene Kloof
Prie Fonteyn
Riebeks Castel
Dassen Eyland
Capoeberg
Bavians berg
Dassen Berg
Paerd Berg
Blaau Berg
Robben Eyland
Paarle berg
Jostenberg
Roeberg
Bottellary
Babylonsche Tooren
Tafel Baay
Tygers Berg
Simons berg
Frans Hoeck
Cap
Saxenbourg
Tafelberg
Duyvels Berg
Rond bosch
Stellenbosch
Constantia
Hout Baay
Steenberg Hoek
Visch Hoek
Hottentot Holland
False Baay
Romans Klip
Simons Baay
Buffels Baay
Hanglip ou Cap False
Cap de Bonne Esperance
Echelle de Toises dont le 34e degré contient

Contents

Introduction

View of a Bushman kraal – W J Burchell.

The 17th Century was a time of great upheaval at the Cape. This era, which saw the founding and rapid growth of a thriving town, also brought destructive changes for the Bushman and Khoekhoe groups who inhabited the area.

The indigenous peoples lived by gathering, hunting and herding. In the first half of the century, these traditional ways of life were not greatly disrupted by the passing European ships that had started to use the Cape of Good Hope as route to the East, occasionally stopping to trade with the locals. However, the arrival of the Dutch settlers in 1652 set in motion dramatic social changes – forever altering the lives of the original inhabitants of the Cape, as well as those who came to the Cape from around the world as settlers or slaves.

The Kaapse Vleck (Cape Town) in the second half of the century was a scene of constant change. Initially, the settlement and its immediate surroundings were inhabited by a handful of Dutch and Khoekhoen, but by 1660 it was a busy port where "all the major languages of the world, African (Bantu and Khoekhoen), Indo-European, and Malayo-Polynesian"[1] were spoken. The vast, sprawling network of the Dutch East India Company needed employees from all walks of life, and the volunteers and crew on board the first Dutch ships headed for the Cape were a motley bunch. Mostly, they were poor peasants and artisans, desperate for a new start.

For women, the rough, rapidly developing settlement held special challenges. Farming was the mainstay of the economy, and women from all walks of life played a major part in expanding agriculture, on a small or large scale. Women's labour was crucial in establishing the Company gardens and farms, as well as privately owned farms and business enterprises. Freed slave women and many free burgher wives supported themselves by starting market gardens, and some proved that they were good livestock farmers. Not only did they supplement their families' meagre incomes, but they were able to supply fresh meat and produce to passing ships.

A common thread links the women who populated the early Cape. They all faced daily

1 Shell, *Children of Bondage*, p xxv.

hardship and danger, whether they were Khoekhoe, Bushman, slave or European. (At this time, there were no other black South African groups resident in the western or north-western Cape.) They bolstered the population, contributing to the expansion of the multiracial settlement. Children were born and families were nurtured, often in strange, dangerous and unfamiliar surroundings. Women from all backgrounds co-existed at the Cape, working together, marrying into each other's families, creating a "tapestry of lives".

One of the fascinating aspects of Cape history is how the genealogies of some of South Africa's best-known families are revealed by tracing the female line. These family trees illustrate the mix of nationalities, creeds and colours that melted into each other to make up the South African population. They also reflect the social, economic and political circumstances of the time. Many slave women, for example, married European men and, like their white counterparts, produced large families and became matriarchs of "white" South African families.

The small population at the Cape thus lived lives that were loosely interwoven – but not on an equal basis. Even though many European women lived in poverty, they had distinct social and economic advantages over the slave women and Khoekhoe servants who worked in their households.

Female slaves formed the backbone of the workforce on private farms and market gardens, in the Company gardens and on Company farms. They also played an important role in maintaining Robben Island, where they kept fire beacons burning to warn ships of danger, herded sheep and gathered shells for use in construction on the mainland. In private homes, settlers became increasingly reliant upon the labour of these subjugated women.

In the early years of the settlement, only a few Khoekhoen worked for the settlers, but towards the end of the 17th century their numbers increased. They were adept at milking, making butter and any other dairy products – all skills that were part of the traditional Khoekhoe lifestyle. Khoekhoe and slave women were also used as nannies, housemaids, wet nurses, seamstresses and cooks.

Working-class white pioneers also had a hard time at the Cape. They had to start their lives over in a strange place – surrounded by wild animals and a wilderness of unfamiliar plants, with unfriendly Khoekhoe neighbours, in a place where desperately needed provisions took five months or more to arrive by ship. They camped out in makeshift tents and huts, built their own homesteads, worked in their homes, and helped out in the fields if they could not afford to buy slaves or hire Khoekhoe servants. The majority of Dutch and German women were from working-class backgrounds and were accustomed to manual labour.

The French Huguenot women, who started arriving at the Cape as refugees in the later years of the century, came from more mixed strata of society: there were peasants among them, but also wives and daughters of skilled artisans. However, most of them had lost their financial assets while fleeing from country to country. They too were accustomed to working in their own homes and fields without the help of slaves or servants.

Despite these hardships, within a decade of arrival many of the Dutch, German and Huguenot women pioneers were mistresses of thriving homesteads and farms, assisted by slave women and Khoekhoe servants.

These women played a vital role in establishing the infant agricultural economy at the Cape. Widows ran farms single-handedly; wives, mothers, sisters and even grandmothers were all involved in the day-to-day running of large farms and households; and many were entrepreneurial, starting canteens, inns and bakeries to boost the family finances. However, it must be remembered that they were handed the means to do so by the Dutch East India Company in the form of credit to buy farming equipment, seeds, oxen and farmland. Slaves and Khoekhoe servants were given no financial assistance at all by the Company.

Despite the increasing number of flourishing farms, constant misfortune – droughts, cattle and crop diseases and bad management of resources – meant that it was a struggle for farmers to provide the Cape residents with enough food to survive, let alone export. Women had their own particular problems: they were expected to marry young and produce large broods of children. At the Cape, the age for marriage was considerably lower than in Europe at the time. Larger families meant a free labour supply when the children were older, but it also meant more mouths to feed. Many European families existed on the breadline, with continual Company aid.

The refreshment station and settlement needed more than agriculture to survive. The constant stream of disembarking travellers, Company officials, soldiers and sailors needed accommodation, food, drink and entertainment. The wives of the Commanders of the Cape had to entertain Company officials at their own expense. Working-class women started canteens, inns and bakeries, much needed in the bustling little Table Bay port. Again, they relied heavily on the labour of female slaves and Khoekhoe servants to keep their businesses running.

Even prostitutes can be said to have played their part in the success of the refreshment station. Men, starved of female company after months at sea, knew that the slave lodge and the harbour housed many available women; the Company turned a blind eye to the thriving sex trade that went on at the slave lodge.

Some women lived in comparative luxury. However, fortunes changed rapidly and wives were dependent on their husbands' money; there was no such thing as a private fortune for a wife. Whatever land or money she brought into the marriage became the property of the husband.

The price of good living at the Cape was usually an arranged marriage, and wives had to make the best of a bad bargain. One factor in their favour was the dearth of European women at the Cape: successive Commanders of the Cape grappled with the problem that the ratio of European men to European women was far too high. Opportunistic European women en route to the East often made hasty marriages at the Cape, and settled down to the hard life of a pioneer wife.

Nonetheless, the Cape women ran huge households with aplomb, entertaining guests with vivacity and generosity. Whether Dutch, German or French, the South African hostesses gained a reputation for warm hospitality.

Women had no voice in the running of the Cape settlement but undoubtedly many men were influenced by their wives' views on the laws that applied there. The Dutch East India Company valued hardworking, entrepreneurial woman settlers. Van Riebeeck appreciated the sacrifices made by the woman settlers and on 5 December 1656 he invited them to a picnic. Simon van der Stel, a later Commander of the Cape who did much to expand the settlement, also recognised their value: he said they were "precious jewels"[2], and were to be treasured.

Whatever their origins, many of the pioneer women – Dutch, French, Khoekhoe, German, from the East or from elsewhere in Africa – were resourceful and possessed great fortitude and strength of character. Although the details of their lives were often not reflected in the official records of the time, they laid the foundation of South African society, culture, and family life. By sketching the lives of a handful of these extraordinary women, *A Tapestry of Lives* honours their contributions.

Author's note

It is difficult to achieve balance in an account of women's lives that spans the pre- and post-colonial eras. Only a smattering of information exists on the lives of women who lived at the Cape before the arrival of the first Europeans. Neither the Khoekhoen nor the Bushmen who were living at the Cape in the early 17th Century left written records. The information we have has been passed down by oral history or in rock art. Some early European explorers left accounts of indigenous women, but these sailors and adventurers knew little about the culture and the language of the Khoekhoen and the Bushmen, and often misinterpreted what they witnessed. Such evidence does not tell us the stories of individual women.

Of necessity, therefore, the chapters on the pre-colonial Bushmen and Khoekhoen deal chiefly with their culture and lifestyle as a group, rather than with personalities. These chapters give a general view of women in these complex cultures, which of course have their own long histories and internal variations; cultures that were irrevocably changed by the arrival of the European settlers.

It is only with the arrival of the Dutch, with their custom of meticulous record-keeping, that the stories of fascinating characters like Krotoa were documented and preserved – albeit from a Eurocentric point of view. With regard to the Dutch, German and French Huguenot women, there is far more official documentation.

Sadly, no individual letters or diaries survive from the 17th Century: the voices of the women themselves are silent. There is only a collection of letters from the early 1700s, written by Johanna van Riebeeck (granddaughter of Jan). But Company records, the writings of Baron van Reede tot Drakestein and Jan Van Riebeeck's journal provide some valuable information on the first woman pioneers at the Cape. Slaves such as Angela of Bengal also formed an integral part of the population at the Cape, and some of these women's stories are told in official documents.

Images of life at the Cape in the 17th century are scarce. For this reason, some llustrations from later eras have been included, where appropriate.

While this book is broadly arranged around particular individuals who fell into different social groups – indigenous inhabitants, settlers, slaves – it is clear that social categories at the early Cape were not always so clear-cut: a few fortunate slaves could become property owners; women fleeing poverty in Europe could end up managing vast estates (or in disgrace on Robben Island); and a Khoekhoe girl could become the progenitor of several influential "white" South African families. Only later did racial and social categories at the Cape tragically harden.

2 Leibrandt, *Precis of the Archives of the Cape: Outgoing Letters*, June 1691.

CHAPTER 1

The Bushman gatherers

Female Bosjesman (Bushman) – S Daniell.

In the early 17th Century, two groups of people lived side by side at the Cape: the hunter-gatherer Bushmen, the original inhabitants of the area, and the Khoekhoe pastoralists, who had moved into the region from the north about 700 years earlier. The major cultural and economic difference between the two groups was that the Khoekhoen owned cattle, but there was a great deal of interaction between them: Khoekhoen and Bushmen intermarried, bartered, co-existed and occasionally fought over game, cattle-poaching and water-hole. Some hunter-gatherers took to pastoralism, and vice versa. (Bartering never happened on a large scale because the nomadic Bushmen did not accumulate goods.)

The Khoekhoen were generally taller than the Bushmen, which can be attributed to their regular supply of protein in the form of meat, milk and butter. Some Bushman groups acquired domestic animals from the Khoekhoen or worked for them temporarily as herders when game was scarce. In the process, the protein in their diet increased, which caused a blurring of the physical distinctions between the two groups. Some historians prefer to class them as one people, the Khoisan.

Unfortunately, there are no first-person accounts of the lives of women at the Cape at this time. Our knowledge of life in the early part of the 17th Century is limited to the accounts of later European explorers – a Eurocentric view – and archaeological evidence. To a certain extent, clues can also be

A European impression of a Bushman family group, dating from 1779.

found in studies of more recent Bushman and Khoekhoe groups, although of course cultural patterns change over the years and from group to group. This chapter and the next, then, offer general overviews of a lost way of life, drawn from these sources.

The Bushman gatherers

Although they had no form of writing, the Bushmen left us valuable records of their everyday existence in the form of discarded clothes, animal bones, household implements, jewellery, hunting equipment, burial sites and the rock art paintings for which they are famous. These artefacts are found in caves and middens dotted throughout southern Africa.

The concept of land ownership by groups or individuals was foreign to the Bushmen. Bushmen groups had loose control of the areas in which they foraged and hunted and found water. In a society notable for its lack of political organization, the only office-bearer was the guardian of the band's right to waterholes and veldkos in a prescribed area. However, even this land was not jealously guarded: in times of drought or famine, groups were allowed to encroach on each other's territory. The guardian of the group's rights to waterholes was rarely a woman, as this honour passed from father to son. Occasionally, if there was no male heir, a daughter would temporarily hold this position, but only until her son was old enough to fulfil these duties.

Bushman bands, linked by kinship, were small: rarely did more than one hundred people roam together, usually fewer. In times of food shortage or for personal reasons, smaller nuclear family groups would break away from the band for a time and perhaps rejoin it later. This nomadic existence was dependent upon the seasonal growth of plants and the movement of game. In addition to using stone tools, they used bone and wood to fashion weapons, clothing and ornaments, and hunted with bows and arrows. Game was plentiful, with the land supporting massive herds of hartebeest, springbok, kudu, eland, reedbuck and buffalo.

Despite this apparent abundance of food, life was hard. In times of drought, or when plant or animal disease occurred, the family had to move to find food elsewhere. It is estimated that a Bushman woman walked an average distance of 2 400 km per year, including daily foraging trips and moves to new locations. A new home might have been as far as 100 km away. Apart from the weight of a baby, a woman would also carry at least 10 kg of household equipment. In 1837, Andrew Smith expressed his amazement at seeing Bushman families on the move: "Every burden is borne by the female, and some not inconsiderable, consisting of implements for obtaining food . . . the men are comparatively unencumbered, only carrying bows and arrows".[3]

Caves were often used as shelters, but not all of them were permanently inhabited. When food and water were not freely available within a reasonable walking distance, the shelter would be used only as a temporary stop-over. Many Bushman bands spent their nights and days in the open veld, with only a temporary shelter fashioned from twigs covered in grass and reeds or made from handwoven grass mats. A hole dug in the ground and filled with grass served as a bed for the entire extended family.

The essential role of gathering

Bushman women played a vital part in the survival of the community. While men hunted for game, the women foraged for veldkos – roots, berries, seeds, fruits, tubers and wild honey. Rock art and accounts from early travellers abound with portrayals of the Bushman men's hunting prowess, but in fact women played a greater role in the daily production of food. Indeed, the Bushmen should be classified as "gatherer-hunters".

Digging through the layers of earth in caves and surrounding areas has revealed the remains of Bushman meals, accumulated over centuries. Meals prepared by Bushman women living along the coastline of South Africa were a feast of seafood, including crabs, mussels and crayfish, as well as seals, penguins, birds, mammals, roots and wild fruits. Ostrich eggs, dassies, mice, termites, larvae, locusts, caterpillars, lizards and snakes were all consumed with relish by the Bushman cook and her family.

Another important women's chore was collecting and looking after the group's water supply, which was stored in ostrich eggshells and bags made from springbok hide. Although women did not hunt larger game, they were extremely proficient in capturing snakes, tortoises, hares, birds and lizards, and also faced danger from predators on their foraging trips. As a protective measure, women usually went out in groups to forage for veldkos. Often they were accompanied by their pet dogs, who offered protection and who were trained to retrieve any small game that was flushed out.

Before a hunt, discussions were held within the group on weather conditions, sightings of game, tracks left by animals and the variety of game in the area. Because women covered vast distances while gathering veldkos and were extremely observant, their opinion on these matters was eagerly sought by male hunters.

3 Smith, *The Journal of Andrew Smith and George Chapman*, p 132.

When game and veldkos were scarce, the Bushmen moved further afield in search of food. Families might move from one place to another for seasonal vegetation, game, or because of drought and disease. Women, with their superior knowledge of where to find veldkos, were consulted on the decision to move.

By sunset, most chores had to be finished, as from then on there would be only firelight. Up at sunrise, a woman suckled her baby, fed the rest of the family, then set off to gather food, often with a small child in tow and a baby strapped to her back.

Rock paintings portray women with digging sticks in their hands as they search for edible roots and tubers. The digging stick was a strong, straight piece of wood, the end of which was inserted into a hole bored into a rounded, heavy stone, and then tied with a thong. The stone served as a weight, enabling the digging stick to grind into the earth, loosening and removing soil around a plant's roots. The long, pointed horn of a gemsbok could also be used as a digging stick.

Bored stones used by Bushman women to weight digging sticks.

Another useful household implement was the honey stick, used to extract wild honeycombs from rock faces and trees. Skin bags rubbed with fat to make them soft and pliable were used to carry and store the honey.

Cosmetics, clothing and jewellery

Rock paintings and, in later years, sketches and photographs by European travellers show Bushman women with beads twisted in their hair. They experimented with hairstyles, using fat and specularite (a shiny stone which was ground to a fine powder for this purpose) to shape, style and add lustre. Sometimes a skin turban was wound around the hair. Cosmetics in the form of red ochre and charcoal were applied to the face and body, for ceremonies, rituals and celebrations. Perfume made from powdered buchu leaves was applied all over the body. A thick layer of animal fat smeared over a woman's face and body served as protection from the blazing sun. Finding a tortoise was a happy occasion: not only could the meat be eaten, but the shell itself could be used to store water or women's cosmetics.

The Bushmen did not cultivate plants, or spin any fibres such as cotton or silk. Their garments were all made of skins or fur. These skins had to be cleaned, scraped, tanned and treated before they could be sewn into garments. The implements the Bushmen used to slaughter animals and prepare the skins were stone cleavers, scrapers, knives, chisels and blades. Wooden pegs and bone knives were also used, as were spatulas and needles for sewing clothes. With these tools, the seamstress created her summer wardrobe, which consisted of skirts of different lengths. Some were minimal, just a flap in front and at the back tied with thongs, while other skirts covered the body from the waist to the calf or thigh. Often decorations of tassels and ostrich-eggshell beads were sewn into the skirt. Sinews, chewed to make them pliable, were fashioned into thongs to sew garments together. In lean times, when food was scarce, women made skin belts worn tight around the abdomen to stop the pangs of hunger.

One essential garment was the kaross. A kaross of thick fur was very practical for the winter, because it could be both a luxurious cloak and a warm blanket at night. Sometimes a Bushman woman would wear a lighter cloak of skin, which could also serve as a bag to carry food on a foraging trip. Fashioned into a sling, this type of kaross was also handy for carrying a baby. A baby sling was lined with soft grasses or other absorbent substances and subjected to regular cleaning and airing. It was adjusted so that the baby could feed easily at the mother's breast.

Both women and men's clothing was decorated with beads, appliqués of skin and sometimes copper. The women's clothing was usually more ornate. Jewellery was also popular and Bushman women made bead necklaces, pendants, bracelets and bands to be worn around the head, ankles and waist. They were extremely inventive and made

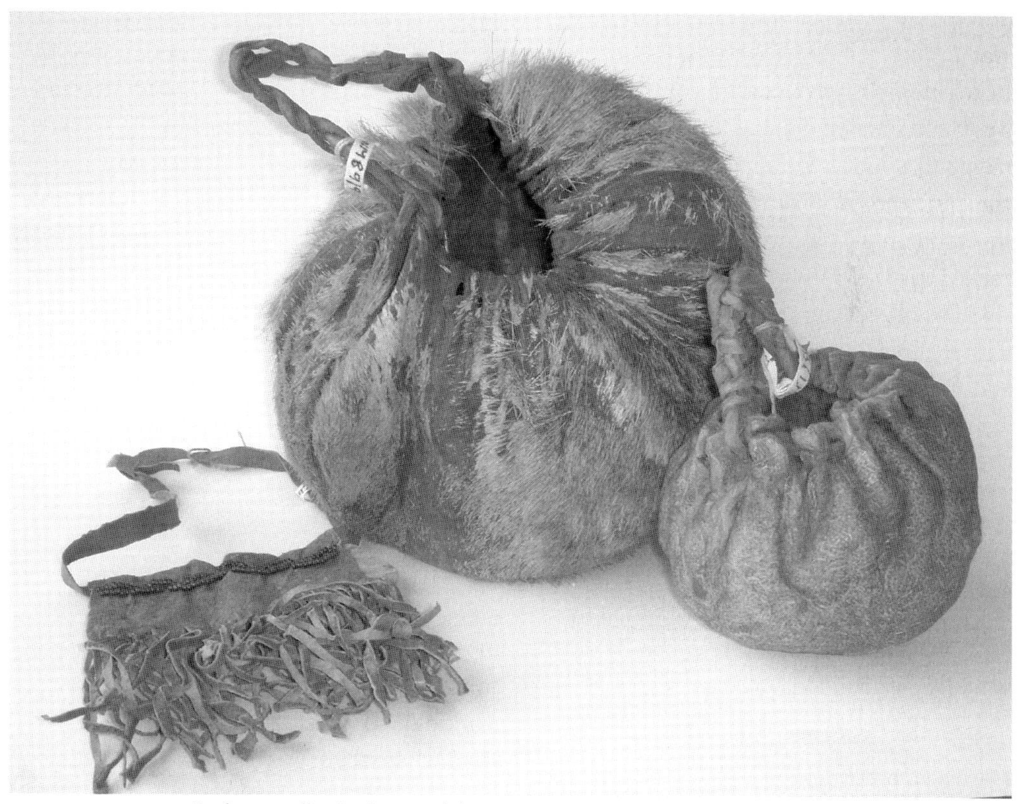

Bushman collecting bags and decorative item in the Wellington Museum.

jewellery fashioned from ostrich eggshell, bone, ivory, tortoise shell, animal teeth and wood. Beads were bartered with passing Portuguese sailors.

The art of body piercing was known to Bushmen women, and was normally part of a ritualistic ceremony. They pierced their ears to insert dangling earrings, which might be intricately made from copper and other metals bartered from the Khoekhoen. They also pierced their noses for pieces of ornate jewellery. Sometimes they painted their bodies to make an outfit more decorative and to make a distinction between everyday and ceremonial events.

Healing rituals

Belief in spirits was a central component of Bushman religion. Shamans or healers, both men and women, could communicate with the spirits, normally during ritual dances, and summon up the power to heal, advise or help the living in some way. In order to heal, the shaman entered a trance to communicate with the spirits. The men would form a circle and dance in time to the clapping of the seated women – clapping and singing were vital parts of the healing process.

When a woman fell pregnant she was thought to lose any magic or healing power she possessed (which might otherwise harm her unborn child). For this reason, the majority of female healers were generally older women, past childbearing age.

Marriage and children

Polygamy was common practice among the Bushmen, and accepted as a practical arrangement. Bushman families often lived far removed from each other and another woman could be a companion, a helper with the workload, a babysitter and a midwife. In areas where there was a surplus of females, men sometimes took four or five wives. This served as a form of protection for women; for an unmarried Bushman woman there was no place in society. Where the numbers

Bosjesman (Bushmen) *frying locusts* – S Daniell.

of female and male were equal, monogamy was the rule.

With their nomadic lifestyle, Bushman women did not rear many children. There was usually a gap of three to five years between births. Having to travel long distances while carrying a baby and all the household belongings, as well as tending to other children, meant it was impossible for a woman to have too many young children at any given time.

Bushman midwives aborted any unwanted pregnancies. If a baby was born during the period when a mother was still breast-feeding another child, the midwives took the baby away before the mother could hear its first cry, and buried it. The midwives also had a

Two older Bushman women wearing karosses. While these women are relatively modern, their clothing is similar to what Bushman women would have worn in the 17th century.

duty to kill a deformed infant; life was hard enough for a healthy child.

Children were loved and well treated. The life of a child was precious and from the toddler stage children were taught by their mothers to identify footprints, so as not to get lost.

The role of older women in the band was extremely important. Apart from being favoured as shamans, they sat around the fire at night entertaining and simultaneously educating children with folklore about the veld and wild animals. These storytelling sessions were invaluable in passing on the culture, customs and knowledge of the Bushman people from generation to generation. Sadly, much of this lore has now been lost to us forever.

1652: Lifestyles changed forever

The destruction of the Bushman way of life began with the coming of the first European settlers. The ability to move freely around the countryside to gather, hunt and use waterholes began dwindling from the arrival of the Dutch at the Cape in 1652.

At first, contact between the Dutch and the Bushmen was sporadic and minimal. By this time, the Khoekhoen had domain over the area around what is now Table Bay, which they used as grazing land for their herds of livestock; the Bushmen had moved further inland, but still made sporadic raids on Khoekhoe livestock.

In 1655 Dutch explorer Jan Wintervogel and his party came across a party of men in the vicinity of the present day Malmesbury who were "very small in stature, subsisting marginally, quite wild, without huts, cattle or anything in the world, clad in skins like the Hottentot (Khoekhoen) and speaking almost as they do".[4] In December 1660, a group of Dutch explorers described the first group of Bushmen they came across as "a poverty stricken band of tiny people". To the Dutch, they seemed poor because they owned no cattle or sheep and had no permanent homes. Their shelters consisted of "low huts made of branches" where "the little fellows will spend the night".[5] The Dutch were surprised that the small group of Bushmen were not interested in trade, but offered the Dutch honey and dried fish – a welcome gift, as the Dutch group were suffering from hunger and thirst.

The Khoekhoen called the Bushmen the Sonqua ("Soa" in some of the Khoekhoe languages means "bush" and "qua" means "people"), and complained to the Dutch that the Sonqua were thieves who stole their livestock and their wives. Bushman hunters earned the reputation of being "fearsome robbers"[6], to the extent that the Khoekhoen even resorted to asking the Dutch (with whom they were not on the friendliest terms) for help against the Sonqua in 1656.

In the early years at the Cape, the Bushmen were of little account to the Dutch Commander Jan van Riebeeck and his settlers. They possessed no cattle, sheep or goats to trade, and they were therefore of no economic value to the Europeans. The Bushmen shared all their possessions and kept these to a minimum to travel easily, so from their point of view there was little need to enter into large-scale trading with the Dutch.

Dutch disinterest in the Bushmen changed, however, when colonists began to move further into the interior towards the end of the

4 Thom, *Journal of Jan van Riebeeck*, vol II, p 49.

5 Thom, *Journal of Jan van Riebeeck*, vol III, p 300.

6 Deacon & Deacon, *Human Beginnings in South Africa*, p 130.

Rock painting from the Clanwilliam area, showing two women.

17th century, cultivating land that had been the domain of the Bushman gatherer-hunters for thousands of years. Still, at first the traditional Bushman way of life was not deeply threatened; despite the encroachment of land-hungry European settlers, the Bushmen were still able to find new hunting and gathering grounds. And, apart from the occasional clash when a few cattle were stolen, the Bushmen did not pose a problem to the first European farmers.

Nonetheless, as land pressure intensified, Bushman groups started moving northwards and eastwards, away from the encroaching Europeans. Many Bushman groups were forced to move to the arid north-western Cape or into the mountainous regions of the southern Cape. The settler population continued expanding, engulfing more and more land.

The trekboer movement, which gathered momentum in the 18th century, posed a far greater threat to the survival of the Bushmen than anything that had come before. Ultimately, the Bushmen would be hunted like vermin by the Europeans, and pushed to the brink of total annihilation.

CHAPTER 2

The Khoekhoe cattle-herders

Khoekhoen dancing and playing musical instruments – P Kolben, 1727.

The Khoekhoen were pastoralists who also gathered and hunted. Khoekhoen means "men of men" (or, in some Khoekhoe languages like Nama and Korana, "people"). Khoekhoe culture and society were built around the ownership of cattle. The accumulation of goods and livestock resulted in an economically based social hierarchy, which had particular implications for the role and status of women.

By the time the first written records mention the Khoekhoen in the 1500s and 1600s, they were spread throughout the Cape. In 1639, Johan Albrecht von Mandelso, a German whose ship was anchored in Table Bay, encountered a Khoekhoe clan they called the "Watermen". These people, whom in 1652 Jan van Riebeeck called the "Strandlopers", were foragers who did not own cattle. In Von Mandelso's opinion the Watermen lived "miserably by the waterside". They existed on "herbs, roots and fishes, and especially on dead whales cast ashore."

Von Mandelso described another Khoekhoe clan, the "Solthanimen", who lived further inland (probably near Saldanha Bay), as a superior clan because they possessed "lovely cattle, sheep and goats". Their cattle and sheep differed from the European breeds in that the cattle had "a large hump" (the forerunners of the hardy Afrikander cattle), and the sheep sported "large fat tails weighing fifteen or twenty pounds".[7] The majority of the Khoekhoe clans owned large herds of

7 Raven-Hart, *Before Van Riebeeck*, p 152.

A party of Khoekhoen riding oxen. Amidst the family's herd of goats and sheep a woman rides on an ox with her baby on her back. The household goods are loaded on a pack ox. This 17th-century drawing is by an unknown artist.

cattle, but disease, drought, stock theft and war sometimes left clans poor, like the Watermen.

Although the Khoekhoen still gathered veldkos and hunted game, their primary source of food was livestock – sheep and, in the dryer areas of the southern Africa, goats. (The only crop they grew was dagga.) Cattle were highly prized as a source of wealth and social status and were only slaughtered on ceremonial occasions. Both sheep and cows provided milk and butter. An adequate supply of water and grazing to maintain these herds was a necessity all year round, and thus the Khoekhoen were seasonal nomads. Whenever grazing in one area was depleted, the Khoekhoe women packed up the belongings of the entire family, including household goods, together with the hut, on the backs of oxen and moved to wherever there was good grazing. The Khoekhoen returned to the same spots every year.

The Khoekhoe women's survival skills were tested to the utmost when a trek to a new pasture was too far for mothers with young babies, the sick and the old. They would have to stay behind while the men and the able-bodied women moved on. Sometimes it was a matter of a few weeks or even months before the rest of the community returned, leaving these women to cope alone, feeding and nurturing the sick, the aged and the young children.

The matjieshuisie

In 1629, Seyger van Rechteren, the sick comforter from the Dutch ship *Wessenan*, and his wife wandered around the Khoekhoe huts on the shore, commenting sarcastically that they were "so 'enormous' that they can pick them up and walk off with them".[8] This was precisely the point of these practical huts, later called matjieshuisies.

Even though the Khoekhoe huts were small and light, travel for Khoekhoe women was not as rapid or as easy as it was for the Bushmen. The pastoralist lifestyle meant more utensils, equipment and containers for milk. Their shelters had to be bigger and stronger because they stayed in one spot for longer. The Khoekhoen also accumulated personal possessions as a sign of social status and wealth.

Women contributed towards building the domed, oval huts, stretching reed mats over a framework of poles. Reeds from the *Cyperus textilis*, commonly known as the "hardehuise" reed, were used in the Western Cape. They were dried in the sun and then woven into large mats, which were bound together using strips of bark. To make a finely woven mat, women pressed the reeds together with their toes while weaving dexterously with their hands. While in summer the hut was a cool, airy shelter from the blazing sun, in winter it became completely waterproof, as the reeds swelled in the damp. For extra protection and also for decorative purposes cattle hides were sometimes laid over the layer of reeds. When it was time to move, the reed mats were rolled up and loaded onto pack oxen.

The sleeping arrangements inside the Khoekhoe huts differed little from those of the Bushmen. The Khoekhoe family also slept in hollows filled with grass, under karosses which were normally made from sheepskin.

The woman's role

The smooth daily running of the community rested to a large extent on the shoulders of the

8 Raven-Hart, *Before Van Riebeeck*, p 128.

A Khoekhoe group pack up camp in this painting by S Daniell.

women. Married women were accorded the name "taras" (translated literally, "ruler of the house" or "to conquer the master"). Although she exercised no public power, the married woman was in total control of her own household. If a man wanted a mere sip of milk he had to ask permission from his wife. In polygamous marriages, each wife was in charge of her own hut and any unmarried children. The taras decided how much meat and milk could be eaten and by whom. If a woman planned to be away from her hut, she left instructions with the children as to what food her husband could eat – he could not help himself.

In public and on journeys the husband

traditionally walked two paces ahead of his wife. In his own hut, however, he could enter only with wife's permission. Rich fathers often set aside livestock for their daughters as a marriage portion. Daughters and wives could inherit livestock from their fathers and husbands, and make decisions on the management of the family herds. Occasionally, women were appointed for temporary periods as regents and even as captains of a group.

However, women were excluded from any public political and legal power. A Khoekhoe settlement consisted of huts around a big tree. In the area around this tree, men gathered to discuss political and legal issues affecting the whole group; women were excluded. Specially chosen meat hung in its branches and women were forbidden to eat these delicacies.

Khoekhoe and Bushman women and children were sometimes captured in battle by wealthier clans such as the Nama (or Namaqua) and forced to work for their captors as servants. The Nama employed numerous servants, many of whom were their own impoverished kinsmen. The women and girls lit fires, cleaned huts, fetched wood and water, babysat, washed clothes and cooked. They also milked cows and goats and tended sheep. The captive servant girls were treated well and often married Nama men or became concubines. Their children were free to leave but usually stayed on to work for their captors. Most Khoekhoe women, however, did their own chores. Even women with servants had to be industrious. If a Nama woman was accused of being lazy, her husband or father beat her with a strap.

Cooking and food

Women were responsible for gathering veldkos, but in addition they were in charge of milking and making butter. Milking the ewes was the women's duty while the milking of cows was often shared between men and women. It was the eldest daughter's responsibility to decide when the cows, sheep and goats were to be milked and who would assist

Khoekhoen living on the banks of the Orange River painted by W Paterson. Note the woman carrying a bag of ostrich-eggshell water containers.

her. This earned the respect of the male members of the family – so much so that her brothers would speak to her only through an intermediary. The most sacred and binding oath any male could take was to swear by his oldest sister's name.

Milk formed the basis of the Khoekhoe diet. Butter was not only eaten but also smeared onto bodies to protect the family's skins from the elements. Wild spinach cooked with butter was a family favourite, and to the Kora group, melted-down butter was a gastronomic treat. Another delicacy was sour milk, which was made by placing leaves of the ebony tree, chewed first by the female cook, in a bowl of milk to let it thicken and turn sour. Buttermilk and butter were made from leftover milk and were used to supplement the diet and smear on the skin.

A Khoekhoe housewife normally possessed only three pots, one for liquids, another for storing roots and veldkos and a third for cooking. The pots had lugs added to them so that they could be tied onto oxen for the next move. Huge ceramic pots stored milk and water, while the cooking pots had narrow conical bases, which sped up the cooking process. Female potters were extremely skilful at shaping earthenware vessels out of clay and water, without a potter's wheel. The most common colours for pottery were black and shades of red, and pots were often distinctively decorated. Ladles and spoons were made from sea shells, tortoise shell and horn. Hardwood was used to make bowls and platters. All these utensils were ornately carved.

Women collected water and stored this precious commodity in ostrich eggshells, bladders and skins, as well as watertight reed baskets and pails.

A popular beverage was honey beer. This brew was considered a luxury item and women were forbidden to drink it; only men and the elderly were allowed this privilege. There was no such taboo on honeycombs themselves and both women and men always carried skin bags over their shoulders on any expedition into the veld in case they came across a hive. Another kind of beer was brewed from wild berries.

All cooking was done on an open fire, which always attracted swarms of flies. Fortunately, only one meal per day had to be prepared. After the chores of milking and herding the animals were completed at around mid-morning, the group ate their main meal.

The menu varied with the availability of veldkos and meat. The Khoekhoe woman was an inventive cook, sometimes combining meat and veldkos in a stew. The meat would be either from game or domestic animals and, like the Bushmen, the Khoekhoe cook added a variety of insects from time to time. Locusts, caterpillars and termites were a great delicacy. Women who lived near the coast added shell-fish and fish to the family's diet, and knew where whales were frequently beached. The men brought home whalemeat and seals for their wives to turn into food and clothing. A favourite meal was porridge made from grass seeds gathered by ants, which the Khoekhoen extracted from large anthills. Whole lambs were sometimes roasted on the fire, as were game, beef and entrails. When it was inconvenient or impractical to light a fire, the family were quite prepared to eat their meat raw. Even when there was a fire, the meat might be just singed. Adults carried raw entrails around their necks for a few days until they dried out and the resulting dried "sausage" was eaten with relish. Tortoises were also a welcome addition to the menu.

While there were taboos for all adults of both sexes on the consumption of hares, fish without scales and sheep's milk, there were additional rules for women. They were forbidden to eat moles, but more important was the taboo on eating meat of the prime-fed sacrificial oxen, which were only slaughtered on ceremonial occasions. And though women cooked the daily meals, men ate separately from their female family members.

Pipe smoking was a popular pastime – sometimes tobacco, at other times dagga. Smoking was a communal pastime and women relaxed in a circle, often in a reclining position, sharing gossip and passing pipes from one to the other for pleasurable puffs.

Clothing, jewellery and cosmetics

Mothers taught their daughters clothes-making, decorative beading and the art of fashioning jewellery. Barrow, commenting in 1791, wrote that the "Hottentot women were fond of finery".[9] The women he saw were weighed down by a wealth of necklaces, bracelets and leg adornments, most of which were made of glass beads. Thongs made from strips of animal hide were also decoratively bound around their legs, but this was largely a protective measure against insect- and snake-bites. Sometimes as many as 50 of these leather rings were worn at the same time. Widows removed a few of these rings to mark their period of mourning.

Two or three skin aprons were tied around the waist and reached down to mid-thigh. These garments were thickly studded with metal buttons, glass beads and edged with pretty shells. A Khoekhoe woman usually went bareheaded but occasionally wore a skin cap.

9 Barrow, *An Account of the Travels of Sir John Barrow*, p 168.

To finish off a woman's outfit, a sheepskin or kaross hung from her shoulders and down her back. The kaross functioned as a blanket and a warm coat and was also used as a ground-sheet on which to sit. Like the Bushman women, the Khoekhoen sewed a pouch to the kaross and carried their babies this way. No shells or metal ornaments were sewn onto the kaross because it was a functional and hardy piece of clothing. It often became so dry and brittle that "the rattling of dry hard skin announce[d] her arrival before you [saw] her".[10]

During the 16th century, glass beads and metal buttons were introduced to the Khoekhoen by European sailors and settlers. Traditional jewellery was made of tortoise shell, sea shells, ostrich eggshell and leather, while ivory was worn by the wealthy. Khoekhoe women normally wore at least ten bracelets below the elbow and several above it. They also wore many necklaces at the same time and from ankle to knee their legs were covered with bracelets.

Khoekhoe women rubbed butter into their skin to keep it smooth and soft. Layers of grease signified that they were wealthy cattle owners, with dollops of butter to spare for cosmetic purposes. The result was that the Khoekhoen reeked of rancid butter, which to the first European sailors who traded with them was strange and unpleasant. British sailor Nicolas Downton, who traded with the Khoekhoen in Table Bay in 1610, declared that the Khoekhoen were the "filthiest" people he had ever met. He complained that besides smelling of sweat, they "augment" the smell by "anointing their bodies with a filthy substance, which I suppose to be the juice of herbs" and which resulted in their bodies smelling like "cow dung".[11] The smell was probably from the strong-smelling buchu, which the Khoekhoen sometimes mixed with the ochre and butter they spread onto their bodies. Dutch seaman Cornelis Claez described the Khoekhoen as "yellowish skinned like the Javanese, smearing themselves with some grease which makes them very ugly, indeed horrible".[12] The Europeans would have been better off if they had copied the example of the Khoekhoen and protected their skins from the harsh African sun.

Sexuality, marriage and childbirth

Several rites of passage involved seclusion. For example, a Korana girl reaching puberty was secluded in a hut with only an elderly woman who had given birth to several children to attend her, and she could only eat meat from a female animal. A girl's release into Khoekhoe society was joyous, a celebration of womanhood. The girl was washed in order to purify her, her face painted, and she was showered with presents.

The virginity of young girls was guarded in many ways. Daughters and sons lived in small huts on either side of their parents' hut. The daughters' dwelling had the smallest entrance, so that the parents could monitor all visitors. Pre-marital chastity was a rule of the affluent Nama clan and if a girl disobeyed this rule she was soundly thrashed by her parents, in the presence of her lover. Thereafter the parents gave him a similar beating, and if his girlfriend was pregnant he was forced to marry her.

Khoekhoe culture protected the sexual rights of its women and children. Rape, incest

10 Barrow, *An Account of the Travels of Sir John Barrow*, p 168.

11 Raven-Hart, *Before Van Riebeeck*, p 48.

12 Raven-Hart, *Before Van Riebeeck*, p 45.

Korah girls by S Daniell, showing two young Khoekhoe women in front of a matjieshuis.

and child abuse were regarded as heinous crimes. In rape cases, the perpetrator's property was confiscated and given to the parents of the victim. The father of the victim, the headman and community elders had the right to thrash the perpetrator to death.

The existence of male homosexuality in the Khoekhoe community was denied, but practised in secret. Female homosexuality was, however, openly acknowledged and accepted amongst both unmarried and newly married young women. Young girls were also taught, on reaching puberty, that masturbation was natural and desirable.

In some clans, the permission of the parents was essential before betrothal. Many clans allowed girls to choose their own marriage partner, but parents still had the final say. Whether the girl or her parents chose the groom, they were bound to select someone from another clan. These suitors were not always strangers as young men often worked as herders for other clans.

The wise old women of the clan were proficient at concocting magic potions and ointments made from powdered locust legs and fat to drive undesirable lovers away, while love potions were made from the insides of ant heaps mixed with herbs.

As soon as a man had earned enough cattle, he could propose marriage to the girl of his choice. A prospective suitor would present the bride's parents with an agreed-upon number of cattle. In some communities, the groom presented his mother-in-law with a cow, a symbol of fertility, and the bride in turn gave one to her mother-in-law. The groom was also required to provide sheep and oxen for the wedding feast, and a pack ox on which to load the wedding presents and the bridal hut.

The slaughter of cattle and sheep marked ceremonial and social events such as weddings. Marriage was a time for joy and feasting. The bride was smeared with the blood and gall of a sacrificial ox, and its entrails were draped around the necks of the bridal couple. The gall bladder was blown up and attached to the bride's hair, after which she was sent to seclusion in a hut draped with the ox's skin.

After the wedding, the bridegroom was expected to live with his in-laws for some time, normally until the first child was born. Then the couple would return to the husband's clan, where they lived for the rest of their lives. A new hut was built for the couple in the kraal of the bride's parents. The bride was excluded from the first three or four days of festivities; then towards the end she was installed in this hut for the night. The following morning, midst much singing and clapping, the groom entered the hut and took his wife, to the raucous encouragement of the wedding guests.

The bride was given cattle, sheep or goats by her parents and her husband. Only the wife had the right to supervise the milking, bartering and slaughter of this herd. All milk, meat and other products from the wife's herd were solely for the benefit of her own hut and children, not to be shared with the other wives. Unlike the Bushman women who shared everything, the wives of wealthy and elite Khoekhoen were accorded special privileges and amassed material goods. The first wife a man married customarily became the chief wife. All visitors and friends of the husband were entertained in her hut, and the chief wife and her children exclusively wore the best skins, karosses and beads.

Concubines were taken by married Khoekhoe men when their wives appeared barren. Some husbands took advantage of this custom by declaring their wives barren on the flimsiest evidence and then taking concubines in several other clans. However, infidelity was frowned upon by society. Although it did not give the wife grounds for divorce, an adulterer was not allowed back into his wife's hut before he apologised to her in public and gave up his promiscuous lifestyle. Adultery was a reason for a wife to return to the clan of her parents for as long as she chose. Concubines were not punished or stigmatised. However, if a concubine bore children she suffered the

A Khoekhoe woman giving birth. Midwives assist, with a large pot, a huge bowl, extra karosses and skins in readiness. After the birth the mother was tightly wrapped in skins and confined in the hut for seven to eight days. At the end of the mother's confinement she went to the stream to wash. This image dates from 1728.

consequences: they were removed from her care and placed in their father's custody for life.

Childless women resorted to the skills of the clan magicians and wise old women. One of the most common cures prescribed for this condition was to slaughter an unborn lamb and tie it around the neck of the patient, who then carried it around for a few days.

Sons were favoured above daughters. Twins were thought to bring bad luck, and if one of the twins was a girl she was buried alive or exposed to the elements to die. A baby whose mother died in childbirth or shortly thereafter was also put to death, as it was considered impossible to raise a motherless baby.

Abortion was secretly practised by women who had unwanted pregnancies. The treatment was to bind the stomach tightly with straps made from animal skins and to drink large quantities of a noxious brew made from boiled urine and faeces of rock rabbit or powdered thorn bush for several days. Khoekhoe men forbade abortions and if discovered a woman was sentenced to forty lashes by the headman and council. Twenty of the lashes could be administered by the husband if he so wished. Any woman guilty of assisting in an abortion was also sentenced to a lashing. No one was allowed to beat a pregnant woman and this crime carried a severe punishment.

A woman in labour was assisted by older midwives. Immediately after the birth, the new mother was wrapped tightly in karosses, irrespective of the outside temperature, until

Khoekhoe women in a gale. Note their karosses and hide leggings. This painting, by an unknown artis

she was bathed in perspiration. These skins were not removed for a period of seven to ten days, during which time she was not allowed out of the hut. When she finally emerged she had to undergo purification, followed by a sacrificial ceremony conducted by other mothers, welcoming her to their ranks.

Newborn babies were not bathed in water. Instead they were smeared with a protective mixture of pounded wild figs, cow dung and sheep fat.

Spiritual life

Ritual and spiritual beliefs played a strong role in healing the body and the mind. Most

probably dates from the end of the 17th century.

Khoekhoe women knew how to pound and mix herbs and other substances into ointments and medicines to keep their families healthy. The specialists in this field, however, were the wise old women. Even the men of the clan respected their knowledge and went to them for advice on health matters, allowing the female herbalists to make incisions in their skin and apply herbs and ointments.

The moon was one of the deities worshipped by the Khoekhoen. At full moon and new moon dances were held in its honour. Like the Bushmen, Khoekhoe men danced inside a circle formed by the women, who sang and clapped to provide the beat for the dancing men. Khoekhoe women sometimes danced, but always in an outer circle around the men. When Khoekhoe women danced they made small steps, swung their hips and thrust out their buttocks. Besides praise dances to the moon, they enacted the herding of sheep into a kraal when threatened by hyenas, and similar daily events. While the men formed a circle to represent the kraal, some of the female dancers took the role of frightened sheep and others performed the role of the predatory hyenas. Musical instruments were also played by women on ceremonial and social occasions. Among these was a musical bow, adapted from a bow and arrow.

1652: Dutch impact on the Khoekhoen

The Khoekhoen's lives were immediately and radically affected by the arrival of the European settlers. Unlike the Bushmen, the Khoekhoen possessed the ingredient most vital to the Dutch for the success of their planned refreshment station: cattle. They had vast herds of livestock within trading distance of the proposed settlement.

The Khoekhoen's cattle made them fair game to the increasing number of provision-hungry crews passing the Cape. The Khoekhoen had had sporadic contact with European sailors since 1488, when the Portuguese rounded the Cape. The Portuguese found the fat-tailed sheep and long-horned oxen of the Khoekhoen excellent fare for sailors starved of fresh food. In exchange the Khoekhoen were offered trinkets, knives and bits of iron. But clashes inevitably occurred, and the Khoekhoen soon acquired a reputation as fearsome, bloodthirsty murderers.

From about 1650, English and then Dutch fleets began to arrive. Their interests lay in India, Java and Sumatra, and Table Bay was an ideal halfway station where the crews could take in fresh water, rest their sick men and barter for fresh meat. Trade between the Khoekhoen and the Europeans flourished, although the arrangement was not always favourable to the Khoekhoen.

Until 1652, all European traders who landed at the Cape had bartered and left. But when the Dutch commander Jan van Riebeeck and his officials arrived, they were there to stay. The lives of the Khoekhoen in the Cape would be changed forever as they were forced into permanent, and often destructive, interaction with the new settlers.

As the free burghers' farms spread ever outward and Khoekhoe herds declined, the men sought employment with white farmers. At first this was on a migrant-labour basis, working for a season and then returning home to their wives and children. This was followed by a phase in the mid-1690s where the entire Khoekhoe family moved onto the farmer's land, but lived in their own huts and usually brought their own livestock with them. Often the wife or daughter would work for the European mistress.

The Khoekhoen became sought-after labour. By the beginning of the 1700s many Khoekhoen had mastered the arts of working in the fields and driving and mending carts; they were already highly skilled at herding and caring for livestock. The Khoekhoen were used to employment as servants: they had worked for Bantu-speakers and for rich Khoekhoe cattle owners. Khoekhoe women taken as war booty had been used as servants in Khoekhoe households, and there was also a long cultural tradition of working as herdsmen for other clans in lean times.

The women and young girls made good employees as cooks, nannies, midwives, servants, milkmaids and seamstresses. They were adept at making butter, buttermilk and other side products of dairy farming, as well as milking cows, and their labour was a vital contribution towards establishing the Cape dairy farms. European women who ran canteens, boarding houses, inns and bakeries also employed Khoekhoe servants.

Female Khoekhoe labour was therefore a vital ingredient in the establishment of the Cape settlement.

CHAPTER 3

Krotoa

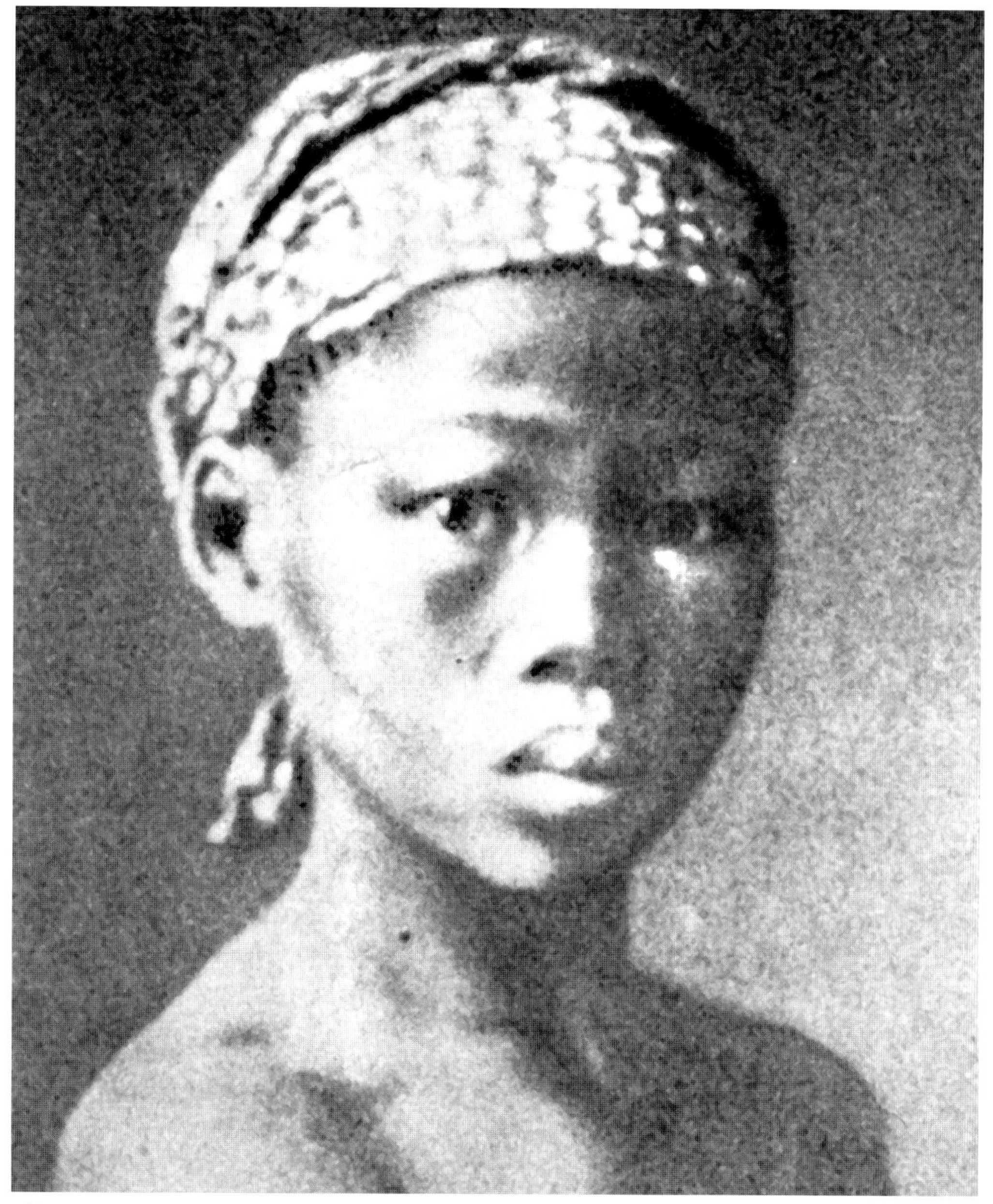

This portrait is popularly thought to be that of Krotoa although in fact the painting is more recent. She joined the Van Riebeeck household as a servant at the age of ten, and became the chief interpreter to the Dutch.

In the latter half of the 16th century, the Dutch began a concerted campaign to wrest the spice trade away from the Portuguese, who were the first to navigate the route around the tip of Africa. In 1602, to achieve this goal, hundreds of small Dutch companies trading with the East were united to form the Vereenigde Oost-Indische Compagnie (the Dutch East India Company). This succeeded in gaining the monopoly on trade from the east coast of the Cape of Good Hope to the Straits of Magellan. The monogram, VOC, was emblazoned on everything the Company owned, from ships to letterheads.

Voyages to the East took many months. Portuguese, English and Dutch ships all stopped off at various points along the southern African coastline to take on fresh water and provisions. One of the most convenient watering places was the Bay of Saldania, later named Table Bay, where streams of fresh water ran down from the mountainside and the indigenous Khoekhoen were often willing to barter their livestock.

Besides being an ideal watering place, Table Bay was a strategically placed point for a Dutch holding midway between Europe and the East. Sailors reported, "The soil in the said valley is very good and fruitful . . . Everything will grow there as well as anywhere in the world, especially pumpkins, watermelons, cabbages, carrots, radishes, turnips, onions, garlic and all other sorts of vegetables." A refreshment station at the Cape could provide a reliable supply of fresh meat and vegetables "for both the sick and the fit of the crews of ships bound for the Indies".[13]

Accordingly, in 1651, a fleet of five Dutch ships set sail from Texel with 90 volunteers and their provisions, to establish a refreshment station at Table Bay under the command of Jan van Riebeeck.

This settlement would profoundly affect the lives of the indigenous inhabitants; not least a ten-year-old Khoekhoe girl, Krotoa, who watched the arrival of the first three Dutch ships, the *Goede Hoop*, the *Dromme-daris* and the *Reiger*, from the sand dunes on the shore.

13 Raven-Hart, *Before Van Riebeeck*, p 177.

The ships that came to stay

Krotoa's uncle Aushaumato was the captain or leader of the Goringhaiconas, a clan that, unlike most Khoekhoe groups, did not own livestock. Drought, disease or theft by other stronger clans had left them dependent on the natural resources of the seashore. The Dutch called them the Strandlopers (beach-combers).

The Goringhaiconas were accustomed to the sight of ships pulling into the bay to take on fresh water, and their crew and passengers bartering for livestock. Aushaumato could converse in the language of the strangers, Dutch, and was prepared to act as an interpreter when the Dutch wanted to bargain with other Khoekhoe clans for livestock.

The initial reaction of the Khoekhoen to the Dutch contingent was reasonably amicable, and trading was brisk. However, some of the Khoekhoe clans over-traded their domestic stock to meet the growing Dutch demand for fresh meat, and began to struggle to replenish their herds. At first trading took place with clans who lived near the newly-built fort, but as these people became less amenable, the Dutch sought contact with those further inland, who were rumoured to have vast herds of fat cattle.

When the Khoekhoen moved their flocks inland for seasonal grazing, the Dutch erected permanent homes on their coastal land. By 1657, when the first nine Dutch farmers were granted farms on traditional Khoekhoe grazing land, it became apparent to the Khoekhoen that the Dutch were about to lay claim to the choicest pastures in the western Cape.

Van Riebeeck quickly became aware of the age-old rivalries between Khoekhoe clans, and sought to play upon them to secure more livestock. His biggest asset in this venture was the remarkable Khoekhoe girl, Krotoa.

A remarkable girl

At the age of ten, Krotoa was employed by Van Riebeeck's wife, Maria de la Quellerie, as a domestic servant. Many Khoekhoe women, at first hesitant to work for the strangers, later became servants in Dutch households. The concept of domestic servitude was not foreign to them: wealthy Khoekhoen also had servants. Equally, the work was not unfamiliar. In both settler and Khoekhoe communities, women were in charge of milking, making butter, cooking, housekeeping and childcare.

Krotoa's interaction with Maria de Quellerie and the Van Riebeeck children earned her the affection of the whole family, and they made every effort to "civilise" her. While on duty in the household she wore East Indian clothing, reserving her kaross for visits to her own people. Krotoa was one of the first indigenous South African people converted to Christianity, upon which the Van Riebeecks changed her name to Eva.

An outstanding gift for languages earned Krotoa the respect of the Dutch. In 1657, when she was only 15 years old, she was a proficient interpreter for Van Riebeeck in negotiations with the Saldhanars, a Khoekhoe clan who lived to the north-west of the Cape settlement. She was fluent in Dutch and also mastered Portuguese – perhaps to a greater degree than the other Khoekhoe interpreter, Doman. On at least one occasion Van Riebeeck called upon Krotoa to translate information he had received from Doman into "better Dutch".[14]

Another asset, in the eyes of the Dutch, was Krotoa's important family connections. Her uncle Aushaumato, known to the Dutch as Herry, was one of the Dutch settler's chief advisors and interpreters. Krotoa's sister, whose name is never mentioned in any of the documentation, was married to Oedassa, the wealthy and powerful chief of the Cochoquas, who possessed large herds of cattle and stock. Krotoa's sister was originally the wife of an opposing chief, Goeboe, from whom she was carried off as a prize of war to marry Oedassa. (This sister may in fact have been a cousin, as the Khoekoen had an intricate kinship system and female cousins were often designated as sisters. The term "mother" also sometimes applied to an aunt, and in this way Krotoa had a "mother" in the Chainoqua and another in the Cochoqua.)

Krotoa's sister, through her marriage to the Cochoqua chief, was an important figure in Khoekhoe history: not only was she Oedassa's chief wife, she was also his favourite and their daughter, Namies, was the apple of his eye. As chief wife she was given every honour and was on several occasions clearly instrumental in affording Krotoa a favourable reception by Oedassa. It was through this sister that Krotoa managed to persuade Oedassa to trade with the Dutch.

The powerful Cochoquas treated Krotoa

14 Thom, *Journal of Jan van Riebeeck,* vol III, p 259.

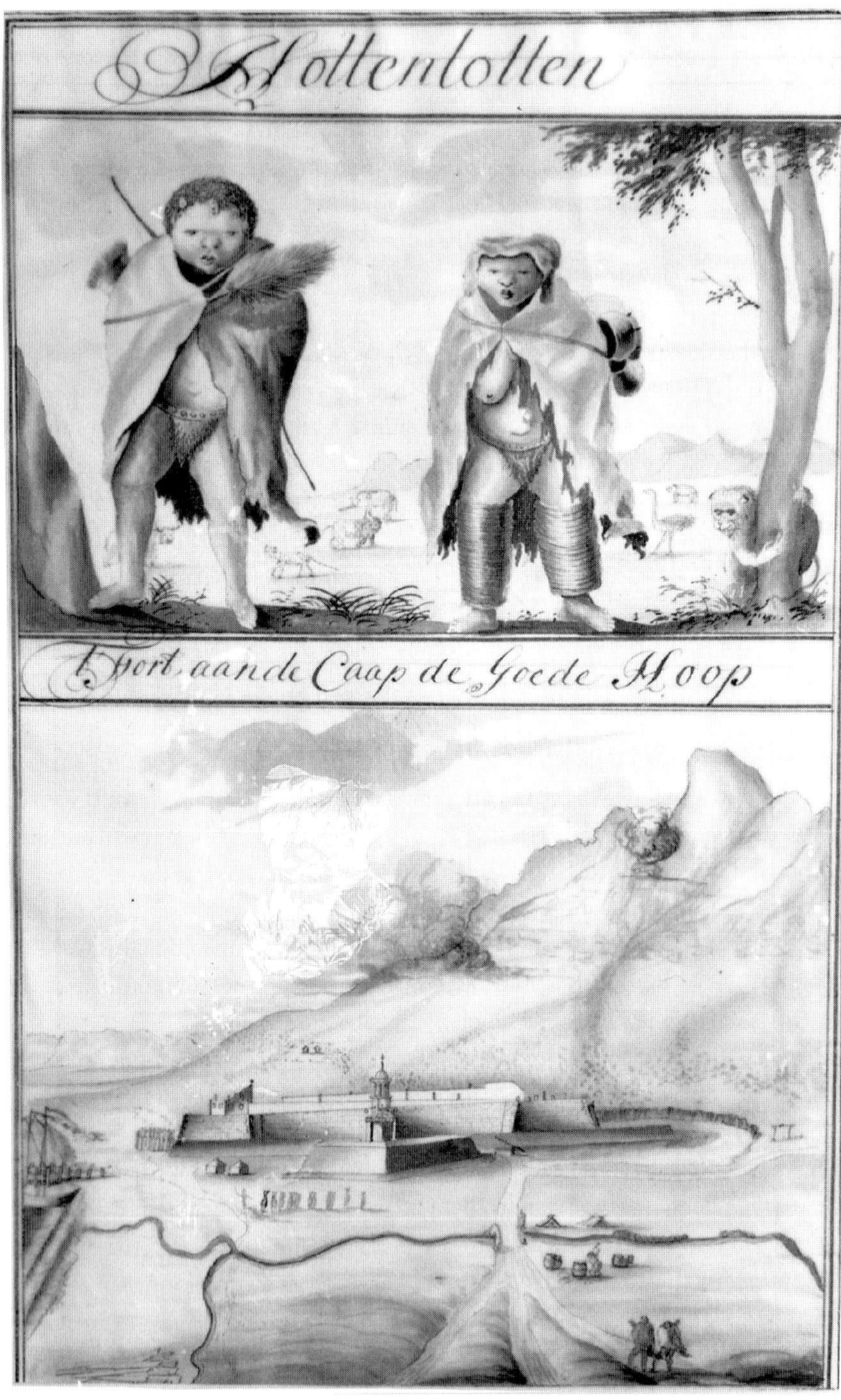

The small wooden fort built by the Dutch became a large stone castle surrounded by a moat. The settlement needed more cattle and the Khoekhoen came in increasing numbers to trade at the castle. Khoekhoe women often accompanied the men on trading expeditions.

with great respect and when she visited them she was allowed to ride on the back of an ox, a privilege reserved for influential visitors. Krotoa ensured that before trading started, gifts of nutmeg, cinnamon, cloves, mace, pepper, strong brandy and the finest tobacco were presented to Oedassa. The Khoekhoen loved music and Krotoa insisted that the Dutch brought fiddlers to the gift-giving ceremony so that the Cochoquas could dance and sing.

There was a strong bond between the sisters. When a Dutch party of traders accompanied Eva to Oedassa's kraal on 22 June 1659, "at the first meeting the two women's joy prevented Eva addressing the other". Eva's sister had been sickly for a long while and the Dutch writer of the journal described her as looking "not altogether well". During the visit the Dutch were touched to note that Eva "perpetually had her arm around the shoulder of her sister, a sign of very great pleasure in each other's company". That night, when the party was gathered around the campfire with Oedassa for an official discussion on trade with the Dutch, "Eva sat leaning on her sister's shoulder."[15] When the news reached the fort on 31 October 1660 that her sister had died, "Eva displayed great grief at the news"[16] and withdrew from her duties at the fort for several days.

On one of his final bartering trips to the fort, shortly before the departure of Van Riebeeck from the Cape, Oedassa brought his daughter Namies to meet the Commander. The Dutch described her as "so pretty, a well shaped girl and no darker than a fairly white mestizo".[17]

In his diary, Van Riebeeck conscientiously listed the goods received by the Khoekhoe traders; those that Namies received on this occasion are comparable to the items offered to other chief traders, indicating that she must have had stock and cattle of good quality to trade. In return for her cattle she received two knives, six bunches of red beads, four pounds of tobacco, half a dozen tobacco pipes, one dozen bead necklaces, four lengths of thick copper wire and five lengths of thin copper wire. Namies' bartering skills demonstrate that Khoekhoe women who owned their own cattle could be a force to be reckoned with. (Although she had no cattle to barter, on this occasion Krotoa received even more goods than did Namies. This was in recognition of her services as interpreter and Dutch envoy to Oedassa's people.) When the Khoekhoe trading party was invited to dine at the Commander's table, Namies was seated at the main table.

On all official and ceremonial occasions, it was Namies who rode at her father's side, and the affection between them was very evident. When he was badly mauled by a lion on a hunting trip, she nursed him back to health, refused to allow any other women near him and sat up night after night to keep watch over him. When Namies fell ill, Oedassa stayed at her side day and night, refusing to go on hunting trips. He even postponed important trading expeditions to the Dutch fort. The Commander repeatedly sent him invitations, but he declined them until Namies had recovered.

Despite her successes, Krotoa was a controversial figure. Wrested from her own society and forced to westernize, she was both respected and mistrusted by the Dutch and by her own people as she sought a balance between her two lives. Although she had "been in the service of the Commander's wife from the

15 Thom, *Journal of Jan van Riebeeck,* vol III, p 78.
16 Thom, *ibid.*, p 247.
17 Thom, *ibid.*, p 267.

beginning",[18] she maintained constant contact with her own people and was bound to have divided loyalties. Dutch approval was unstinting when she denounced runaway slaves who were sheltered by the Peninsular (or Kaapmans) clan, but this made her unpopular with some Khoekhoen – especially when she advised the Dutch to take hostages from the Kaapmans, including the chief's son. Doman, the other Khoekhoe interpreter, openly labelled her a traitor to her own people.

However, most of the information she passed on to the Dutch was to the benefit of her own clan. Krotoa and her uncle Aushaumato were from an opposing group to that of Doman, and they tried to discredit him and his clan in the eyes of the Dutch. The slave harbourers, the Kaapmans, were also at odds with Krotoa's clan, and actions against them were revenge for past cattle raids and kidnapping of women from her own people.

Krotoa's loyalty to the Dutch and her moral integrity led to her denouncement of her uncle Aushaumato (for involvement in the murder of a Dutch herd boy, the theft of Company cattle and copper, and persuading the Khoekhoen not to trade with the Dutch); but when he was imprisoned and sentenced to death by the Dutch, she alone of all the Khoekhoe interpreters and servants at the fort pleaded for his release.

A group of Khoekhoe women relax and smoke

Krotoa was a successful envoy to Oedessa, her powerful brother-in-law and chief of the Cochoquas, and to other far-flung clans. As a result of her efforts "many strange Khoekhoe arrive[d] to barter"[19] at the fort. She also impressed the Dutch by bringing nine Cochoqua men to the fort to be converted to Christianity, and she wanted Khoekhoe children to be educated. But the Dutch did not trust her unequivocally. Officials noticed that when Krotoa acted as interpreter for those whom she favoured, she was inclined to do so selectively, changing the subject when something was said that would not meet with Dutch approval.

They also accused her of an overly vivid imagination, and of telling them exaggerated

18 Thom, *Journal of Jan van Riebeeck*, vol II, p 170.
19 Thom, *ibid.*, p 349.

pipes in this 17th-century drawing. Note the interaction with a Dutch settler on the right.

stories. Westerners had long believed in the legend of the fabled land of Monomotapa, situated somewhere in Africa, where gold and precious stones could be picked up from the sand and the citizens (who were white) all lived liked kings. Krotoa told Van Riebeeck that there was indeed a kingdom to the north whose rich inhabitants were white, kept many black slaves, lived in stone buildings, were ruled by a great king and practiced a religion similar to Christianity. However, none of the Dutch expeditions to the north yielded any evidence of any such kingdom. (It is possible that this legend originates in the great gold-producing strongholds of Zimbabwe and Mapungubwe, which flourished in earlier centuries.)

Krotoa cannot be blamed for this glamorous story; it seems to have been a legend amongst the Khoekhoen as well as the whites. A Khoekhoe man told Van Riebeeck that he also knew of this land, that his wife had in fact been born there and still possessed many of the precious jewels from her homeland. Whenever he was asked to bring his wife with her jewellery she was always too ill or had been attacked and robbed. Krotoa's story was therefore not a figment of her imagination but a legend the Khoekhoen, the Portuguese and the Dutch all believed.

With the introduction of Khoekhoe servants to Dutch households, there was often jealousy between the free servants and the slaves. Krotoa was held in high esteem and affection by the Van Riebeeck family and the Company, but she was jealous of Maria of Bengal, who at one time was a favoured Company slave. Krotoa probably feared that Maria would steal her limelight. In a particularly vehement argument, Krotoa grabbed a pair of pliers and an axe from Maria's hand instead of asking politely for the tools, and then proceeded to hit Maria on her buttocks – a sign of contempt among the Khoekhoen. Krotoa knew that her aggressive behaviour towards a valuable slave would be punished, so she fled to the safety of her own people until the fracas died down. (In 1657 a Company official warned Van Riebeeck that the slaves he owned were illegal – only the Company could buy slaves or accept them as presents. Maria of Bengal was hastily sold to a Company official. Maria later converted to Christianity, was freed and married Jan Sacharias, a Dutch burgher; when her daughter Mary was born, the child was christened at the fort.)

In comparison to the women who lived in the poorer Khoekhoe clans, the Khoekhoe servants employed at the fort were well fed and clothed. But they were isolated in a foreign culture, with no societal support system. Sara, one of Krotoa's contemporaries, committed suicide by hanging herself at the age of 24. She was pregnant, carrying a child fathered by a white man who had promised to marry her, but reneged. Like Krotoa she was fluent in Dutch and able to converse in Portuguese, but she had not been used as an interpreter.

Because she was considered a Dutch subject, Sara was not allowed a Khoekhoe burial. Traditionally, the Khoekhoen buried their dead in an upright position and protected the body against falling sand and stones. Instead, Sara was "to be dishonoured like a European",[20] which meant that she was not buried in hallowed ground even though she was a Christian. After being dragged through the streets her body was tied to a pole and left as food for the birds of prey.

The first Khoekhoe-Dutch war

All Krotoa's intercessions in favour of her people could not avert the rising tide of confrontation between the Dutch and the Khoekhoen. As the VOC allocated more farms to free burghers, they encroached further into traditional Khoekhoe grazing land. Furthermore, these free burghers were stock farmers, and were naturally given preferential treatment over the Khoekhoen when trading with the Company. Khoekhoe clans raided Dutch cattle in the same way that they had always raided rival Khoekhoe clans' stock – an age-old tradition. The free burghers retaliated, and were not above raiding Khoekhoe herds to augment their own.

The traditional cycle of Khoekhoe power

20 Elphick, *Kraal and Castle*, p 184.

structures was broken. In the past, one clan would build up power and herds through raids on its neighbours. After a few years, a strong new leader from another clan would wrest that power away in the same way. Often the cycle of power also depended upon ecological factors such as drought, poor pastures and stock diseases. There would be a natural upswing and recovery as the weather conditions and grazing improved. The advent of the Dutch traders and farmers broke this cycle because they tried to prevent inter-clan cattle raids and skirmishes. The Khoekhoen also had less land for alternative grazing if weather conditions were against them, and therefore had less chance of rebuilding ailing herds.

Khoekhoe clans living in and around the Cape Peninsula, known collectively as Peninsulars or Kaapmans, were the first to suffer. These clans had never been wealthy stockowners, and due to constant over-trading and the creeping degradation of choice pastures, their herds dwindled. Despite approaches from Khoekhoe leaders pleading for the return of their traditional grazing lands, Van Riebeeck refused to act. He said there was more than enough land for all. To the Khoekhoen there was only one option left: war. They had to drive the settlers off their land.

The mastermind behind the first attack was Doman, Krotoa's old enemy, whom she had ousted from the post of chief interpreter to Van Riebeeck. In 1659, the first Khoekhoe-Dutch war was ignited when it became clear to Doman that the Dutch were not only encroaching on Khoekhoe land, but were also preparing to move further inland to trade with Krotoa's relatives, the Cochoquas, and so break the trading monopoly held by the Peninsulars.

Doman had spent enough time within the fort's walls to appraise the weapons used by the Dutch. He launched his attack when the first heavy rains of winter fell in May 1659. The result was as could be expected. The soldiers and the settlers struggled to load their clumsy matchlock muskets with the damp gunpowder, and when they finally succeeded, the guns frequently failed to fire. The Khoekhoen attacked in small groups of about 20 to 60, who were able to dodge and hide for cover and escape the inaccurate and sporadic firing from the troublesome muskets.

The Khoekhoen kept up this intermittent guerilla warfare throughout 1659 and into the first few months of 1660. Each time they struck with lightning speed. They decimated the settlers' crops and stole most of their cattle and sheep. The wives and children of the free burghers fled to the safety of the fort, while the men attempted to guard their farms with the assistance of their slaves and loyal Khoekhoe servants.

The hostile Khoekhoen were unwilling to storm the fort under the concentrated firepower of the soldiers and the free burghers. Yet their ongoing attacks made the Dutch resort to arming their slaves, causing the war to drag on until April 1660. By then both parties wanted peace: the free burghers wanted to return to their farms and the Khoekhoen had meanwhile lost the profitable trade with passing ships. Doman had failed in his attempt to get Krotoa's powerful uncle, Oedessa, to join in the war. The weaker clans were forced to make peace with the Dutch and Doman was discredited among the Khoekhoe groups.

The clans who were allowed to return to trade and graze near the Cape settlement would become Dutch subjects. Although the war left the Khoekhoen in the area around the Cape settlement richer in cattle, it had stripped them of their independence.

Krotoa's decline

Sadly, Krotoa was abandoned by her own people and fell out of favour with the Dutch. The relationship which Krotoa formed between Oedassa and the Dutch officials at the Cape was on a strong footing by the 1660s, and Oedassa felt he no longer needed her as an envoy. In addition, his wife had died and this broke the kinship bond with Krotoa. In 1662 the Van Riebeeck family, to whom Krotoa was emotionally attached, left for Batavia. The next Commander, Zacharias Wagenaar, informed her that her services as an interpreter were no longer in demand, as many Khoekhoen now spoke passable Dutch. Wagenaar disliked Krotoa and called her "a lewd vixen".[21]

For Krotoa there was now no close family or clan support. Tragically, she turned to alcohol and prostitution – one of the earliest recorded cases of prostitution at the Cape.

Prostitution was uncommon in traditional Khoekhoe society, as strong kinship ties normally provided for those who were poverty-stricken and prevented them from straying outside the clan. One of the benefits of polygamy, which was practiced by the Khoekhoen, was that a lone woman was not left to fend for herself. Contact with white men usually took place only on trading expeditions, where the women were surrounded by family and friends.

However, as the Dutch settlement grew, so did prostitution, becoming the only means of support for many destitute Khoekhoe women. By 1686, several Khoekhoe clans within the radius of the Cape settlement had overtraded their stock and their lifestyle was beginning to disintegrate. Barter with the whites had become routine. Khoekhoe men sometimes acted as pimps, offering their wives' services as prostitutes in return for as little as a roll of tobacco. The advent of prostitution led to the introduction of venereal disease, which until then was unknown to the Khoekhoen.

Despite her troubles, in 1664 Krotoa married Peter van Meerhof, an educated 27-year-old Danish man who practiced as a surgeon. He was an accomplished explorer, having accompanied six expeditions to the north-western Cape as official journal keeper, and was an expert on the lifestyle of the Khoekhoen. This was the first marriage recorded between a Khoekhoe woman and a white man. It was presumably a love match, and there is speculation that Van Meerhof was the father of Krotoa's two children born before their marriage. In all, she bore three children during her marriage to Van Meerhof.

The Dutch East India Company paid tribute to Krotoa for her years of service by providing her with a wedding feast at the Commander's house and giving her a wedding present of 50 rix dollars.[22] Considering that her husband's salary was 15 rix dollars per month, this gift showed that the Company still held her in great esteem. And indeed, the Dutch held Krotoa up as a role model to other Khoekhoe women, an example of how successful they could be if they were baptised, "educated" and "civilised" – in other words, became obedient servants of the Dutch.

On the other hand, it is recorded that the

21 Boonzaier et al, *The Cape Herders*, p 75.

22 Several currencies were in use at the Cape at the time, including the rix dollar, the guilder and the real.

Idealised portrait of a Khoekhoe woman consorting with a sailor beneath the Dutch flag. Although published in 1820, this illustration demonstrates the attitudes of many male VOC employees towards the local women at the 17th-century Cape settlement.

Company felt that it owed her at least the 50-rix-dollar wedding present because she had rendered services as an interpreter for many years and had only received food, clothing and accommodation in return. Seen in this light, it was actually a meagre gift.

As part of their wedding present, the Company promoted Van Meerhof to the post of overseer of the prisoners on Robben Island – a gesture that caused Krotoa great unhappiness. While her husband busied himself with the challenges of his new job, Krotoa pined in the solitude of the island. Accustomed to the bustling fort and busy port life, where she had constant contact with her own people, she again fell into depression and resorted to alcohol. There is evidence of her bringing one of her children to the fort in Cape Town to be baptised during this period.

The occasional trip was not enough for her. In a state of intoxication she fell down a flight of stairs and sustained a serious head wound. Krotoa's addiction to alcohol was by no means unique; it had become a growing problem among the Khoekhoe people. In 1668, after only four years of marriage, Van Meerhof was sent to Madagascar on an exploratory trip, where he was attacked and killed by local inhabitants.

At first his widow was well treated by the Company. They gave her and the children a small plot with a house. Krotoa inherited Van Meerhof's male slave, Jan Vos. She was still a valued member of society at the fort and received frequent invitations to dine at the Commander's table. Unfortunately, the old addiction to alcohol took hold again and she returned to prostitution. At that time, punishments were harsh: after she had foolishly insulted the Commander at an official Company dinner, he banished her to Robben Island. The Company terminated her ownership of Jan Vos and the Church assumed custody of him.

Desperate and inebriated, she stripped her children naked and offered all their clothes and the household bedding to a group of Khoekhoen living in the dunes near the fort, in return for tobacco. She then fled in terror to escape exile to Robben Island. Krotoa's children were put in the care of a deacon of the church.

The following day, the children were removed by the Church council and for some incomprehensible reason placed in the care of a woman with the most unsavoury reputation: Barbara Geems was the alleged owner of a brothel and a known prostitute. For Barbara the money the Church paid for the care of Krotoa's children must have been welcome, her husband being a shiftless layabout who relied on his hardworking wife to support the family. Although the Company was reputedly "colour blind", the rest of the small white population probably was not; Barbara may have been the only woman prepared to care for children of mixed race.

Krotoa was soon arrested and taken to Robben Island, where she died five years later. Because Krotoa had died a natural death, unlike Sara, she was accorded a Christian burial in the small church attached to the recently completed castle.

Krotoa's legacy

Three years after her mother's death, Krotoa's daughter Pieternella and her two other children were placed in the care of one Bartholomeus Borns, who signed forms of apprenticeship for the children and contracted to look after and educate them. He and his wife moved to Mauritius, taking the children with him. One of Pieternella's brothers eventually returned to the Cape, where the young man died as a result of "wild habits".[23]

Pieternella van Meerhof also married a European, the Dutch-born Daniel Zaijman. This was a common pattern at the time – children of mixed marriages normally married into white families, which, within two to three generations, tried to erase the traces of their slave or Khoekhoe roots.

Pieternella became a respected matriarch. Zaijman at first struggled to make a living, but eventually became one of the wealthiest plantation owners on Mauritius. When the VOC ordered the evacuation of Mauritius, the couple returned to Stellenbosch with their eight children, founding the Zaijman (Saayman) family in South Africa. One of Pieternella's daughters was named Eva (Krotoa's Christian name). Another daughter, Magdalena, married Johannes Bockelberg, a German, who practiced as a surgeon in Mauritius. After her death, her family settled in Stellenbosch. Krotoa's genes flow through branches of the Bruyns, Botma, Buys, De Vries, Oosthuizen, De Witt, Redelinghuys, Van der Vyver, Theron, Opperman, Erasmus, Smit, Botha, Van den Heever, Huisamen, and Engelbrecht families.

One of Krotoa's contemporaries, a Khoekhoe woman called Cornelia, who also worked as a servant for the Van Riebeecks, had a happier life. She returned to her home kraal after the departure of the Van Riebeeck family and was accepted back into her family. When Johanna Maria van Riebeeck, granddaughter of Maria de la Quellerie, landed in Cape Town in 1710, she visited Cornelia in her kraal near the castle. Her reports were glowing: a stately woman in her 80s, healthy, intelligent and still able to converse in fluent Dutch.

23 Böeseken, *Jan van Riebeeck en sy Gesin*, p 29.

CHAPTER 4

Company wives

Departure of the Company's fleet, showing Amsterdam in the background – De Vroom, 1636.

Despite the 17th century being called the Dutch Golden Age, poverty in the Netherlands was rife. The Eighty Years' War, which ended in 1648, had left many widows and orphans, and unemployment was widespread. The majority of women sailing with Van Riebeeck were working-class, and seeking a better life.

But there were also a few well-off women aboard: the wives of higher-ranking VOC officials, who would form the backbone of Cape "high society". The lives of these privileged women and those who succeeded them, although not always easy, were far removed from the toil of the women who served them. The Commanders' wives came from comfortable middle-class backgrounds, and arrived at the Cape cushioned, to some extent, against the harshness of life there. While free burgher women struggled to put food on the table, the choicest fruit and vegetables would have found their way to the Commander's kitchen.

These women relied heavily upon the labour of slave women and Khoekhoe servants, without whom they would not have been able to entertain on a large scale or carry out many of their official duties.

Maria de la Quellerie – "everybody likes her"

One of the most famous of all early colonial figures was Maria de la Quellerie, the wife of Jan van Riebeeck. When the 19-year-old Maria married Van Riebeeck, she had no inkling that she was destined to play a role in the history of South Africa. The wedding took place on 28 March 1649 in Amsterdam. The pretty Maria, with her sparkling brown eyes and dark blonde hair, married a man

Maria de la Quellerie (van Riebeeck) – Dirk Craey, 1650. Her dress shows that she is the wife of a wealthy man: the collar is snow white and starched, edged with handmade lace. There are jewels in her ears and at her neck and pearls on her cap, which is made of brocade and velvet.

who was ambitious and adventurous – but also in disgrace. He had been sent back to the Netherlands from Batavia because he had been involved in private deals, which was forbidden to employees of the VOC. Maria, on the other hand, came from a respectable middle-class background. Her father was of French Huguenot blood and a minister in the Dutch Reformed and Walloon churches in Rotterdam.

When Van Riebeeck accepted the post as Commander of the Cape, he hoped that the Cape would be a stepping-stone to a better-paid and more powerful position in Batavia. He and all the top officials who followed after him at the Cape put in frequent requests for promotion to the East. Maria must have sailed to the Cape with high expectations of this new venture.

On 14 December 1651, she stepped on board the *Drommedaris* and set sail for Africa. Five weeks earlier she had given birth to her second child, Lambertus. Soon after Lambertus's birth her firstborn son, Anthony, died. The long voyage to the unknown ended on the 6 April 1652, when the *Drommedaris* and the *Goede Hoope* sailed into Table Bay.

The following day a third ship, the *Reiger*, arrived. These three ships carried the Dutch pioneers. Two further ships, heavily laden with the bulk of the provisions, arrived only on the 7th of May, 1652.

Although the journey from the Netherlands to the Cape was made in record-breaking time, it still took about four months in cramped, airless quarters. As the wife of the Commander, Maria had more spacious accommodation than most of the passengers, who were crammed into communal living quarters, but conditions on board ship were not pleasant for anyone.

Living conditions ashore were little better. Compared to the solid buildings and fairly comfortable way of life in their motherland, the first European women found that life at the Cape was rough and difficult. The Cape was a great leveller: even the Commander's family lived in tents or temporary wooden sheds. Construction of the wooden fort took longer than expected; the basic shell and a few rooms were only ready by June 1652, two months later.

It was planned that on completion of the fort, Maria and her family would be the first to take occupation. However, the first inhabitants of the fort were not Commander Van Riebeeck and his family, as it turned out, but the sick comforter and his wife, who was nearing the time for the birth of her first child. She was probably only allowed this privilege because she was the wife of a Company official. (In the absence of a resident minister at the Cape, the sick comforter preached sermons, held religious services, administered to the spiritual needs of the settlers and visited the sick. He was not permitted to perform any of the sacraments of the church such as marriage or baptism.) The move occurred just in time: the day after taking possession of their quarters in the fort, she gave birth to her baby, Benert Willemsz Wiljant, the first child of European origin born in South Africa.

Simply living day to day in the primitive settlement was a daunting challenge. The death rate was extremely high. In the close quarters of the fort, infectious diseases swept through the community like wildfire. Newborn babies were the most at risk. Even when the gardens were well established and supplying fresh fruit and vegetables, and when living conditions in the fort improved slightly, infant deaths were regularly recorded.

Disease claimed rich and poor alike. In the first two months, all the tents and the food-supply sheds flooded during weeks of lashing rain. Clothing, bedding and household supplies were saturated and the food supplies brought out from the Netherlands began to rot. Disease followed in the wake of malnutrition. Almost all the small settlement's inhabitants, including Maria, suffered from dysentery. Many of the soldiers and sailors had scurvy as well. There were several deaths, but Maria and her young son survived.

On 8 December 1655, two babies were born. Maria de la Quellerie gave birth to a son, Anthony, and Gertruuit van der Stael, wife of Frederick Verburgh, had a daughter. The

Verburgh's little girl only lived ten days; Maria's son, her fourth child, died on the 26 February 1656. There was no minister resident at the Cape at the time and an added grief to the devout Maria must have been the fact that the child had not been baptised. Her third child, Abraham, born on the 18th September 1653, survived, as did Lambertus. Thereafter, Maria gave birth to three daughters at the Cape: Maria, born in June 1657, Elisabeth in September 1659 and Johanna in January 1662.

One of Van Riebeeck's priorities at the Cape was to establish a garden to supply fresh produce to passing ships. Maria took a keen interest in the Company Garden from its inception – although she would not have worked in it herself – and was delighted to pick the first two lemons.

According to Bishop Etienne, a Roman Catholic priest who was among the crew of the stranded vessel *La Marchele* and who stayed at the Cape with the Van Riebeecks for ten months, Maria de la Quellerie was the perfect wife for the new Commander of the fort. Maria was an intelligent and cultured woman who was also fluent in French and Dutch. She was therefore able to converse with the many passing Company officials and visitors, whom she had to entertain as part of her duty as wife of the Commander. In Etienne's opinion, she was a wise woman with a calm and confident manner, making the right decisions in often very difficult circumstances. In small congested settlements like the Cape scandal and jealously often arose, but Maria, according to Bishop Etienne, was "indisputably one of the most perfect women I have ever seen and everybody likes her".[24]

Her only weakness was that she was not a Catholic. He forgave her this because she was pious, warm, generous and even-tempered. Bishop Etienne remarked further, "apart from her religion – I have never noticed the least passion in her, though I have often visited her. Whatever business or occupation she had to attend to, she showed so much self-restraint that she never seemed harassed, even not in a few discussions I had with her, for she is the daughter of a minister in Rotterdam and well versed in the Holy Scriptures. She is not opinionated and that is rare."[25]

Van Riebeeck's tenure at the Cape earned him another step up the Company ladder: he was promoted to the post of governor of Malacca – probably his goal from the beginning of his term of office. From Bishop Etienne's report on Maria, it appears that she played a part in this promotion. In May 1662 the Van Riebeecks left the Cape for Batavia, where Maria bore another daughter, Antonia, on the 6th November 1663.

Having survived the exigencies of pioneer life at the Cape, Maria died two years after arriving in Batavia, at the age of only 32. She suffered a miscarriage at six months and a few days later contracted smallpox.

Marie Wagenaar: a social butterfly

Commander Zacharias Wagenaar, his wife Marie and their widowed daughter-in-law arrived at the Cape on 2 April 1662 to take over the post to be vacated by the Van Riebeecks. At first glance, Marie appears not to have been a steadying influence like her predecessor, but to have led the life of a social butterfly, addicted to good food and entertainment, pampered and spoilt. For a household of three people, she was served by no fewer than ten slaves.

24 Thom, *Journal of Jan van Riebeeck*, vol I, p xxv.

25 Picard, *Masters of the Castle*, pp 28-29.

This drawing, c. 1680, depicts Dutch gentry in Batavia. These slave-owners are wealthy enough to have a slave to shield the lady's skin from the sun.

The Wagenaars regularly entertained guests. One of Marie's duties in helping her husband through his term of office was to entertain local officials, passing ships' captains and travellers on their way to and from the East. It was not always a pleasant duty: the Wagenaars complained that they were treated like mere inn-keepers by many of their guests. The Commander footed the bill for entertainment out of his own allowance. On one occasion, gluttonous guests not only devoured all the food, but helped themselves to linen, cutlery, silver and glasses.

Zacharias was not very happy at the Cape. Constantly plagued by poor health, he found his duties arduous. Marie became a source of strength to him – someone he could rely on when Company officials turned a blind eye to his problems. Tragically, on 14 June 1666, during dinner, she developed severe dysentery, and died later that night. Her husband, who had reluctantly stuck out his tenure as Commander, was unable to bear conditions at the Cape without his helpmate. He applied for a transfer to Batavia and was granted one.

Portrait of a lady – Peter Nason, c. 1646. Elaborate hairstyles and adornments were popular among wealthy women, and pearls were particularly admired.

Margaretha van Quelberg: ladylike airs

Whereas Maria de La Quellerie gained respect from the community for her role as wife of the Commander of the Cape, Margaretha van Quelberg and her husband Cornelius were criticised for almost every move they made from the time they arrived in 1666.

Born into a family of wealthy traders in Batavia, Margaretha probably played the part of the first lady to the hilt, flaunting her fine clothes, jewellery and position, an unwise attitude in a community where the majority of women struggled to put enough food on the table for their families. Her ladylike airs drew scorn from the free-burgher women.

Margaretha realised that to make progress at the settlement, the Dutch had to make an effort to communicate and relate to the Khoekhoen. She undertook a journey to the neighbouring Khoekhoe clans to study their customs, and the Khoekhoen were impressed with her efforts. But there was gossip in social circles at the Cape that the first lady had "lowered" herself to lift her voluminous skirts and squat on her haunches, Khoekhoe style, to barter. Despite her supposed loss of dignity, she returned to the castle with more sheep and cattle, bargained from the Khoekhoen, than any of the male officials had ever brought back.

Margaretha's husband executed his duties unsatisfactorily. In June 1668, ignominiously dismissed, the Van Quelbergs set sail for Batavia. It was Margaretha who rescued some of the Quelbergs' reputation – it was presumably due to Margaretha's illustrious family connections that Cornelius was able to keep a position in the Company and in 1669 become a magistrate in Batavia.

Aletta van Hinloopen: the castle-builder

The castle in Cape Town is a national heritage site, but few people know that women contributed to its construction. Aletta van Hinloopen was married to Commander Johan Bax van Herenthals, who was instructed to finish building the fifth bastion of the castle. In 1666, work had started on replacing the wood and mud fort built by Van Riebeeck with a larger, fortified stone castle. The construction of the castle with its five ramparts was a laborious process, carried out under the supervision of successive Commanders of the Cape.

In November 1676, when the rebuilding of the castle did not proceed on time, Aletta joined her husband in setting an example to the local burghers and their wives. On the first day of building, while her husband carried twelve baskets of sand and stones, she managed six in the sweltering heat. Even her seven-year-old son carried his small buckets of sand and stones. The hard labour was not in vain and soon many burghers and their wives followed Aletta's example and joined in.

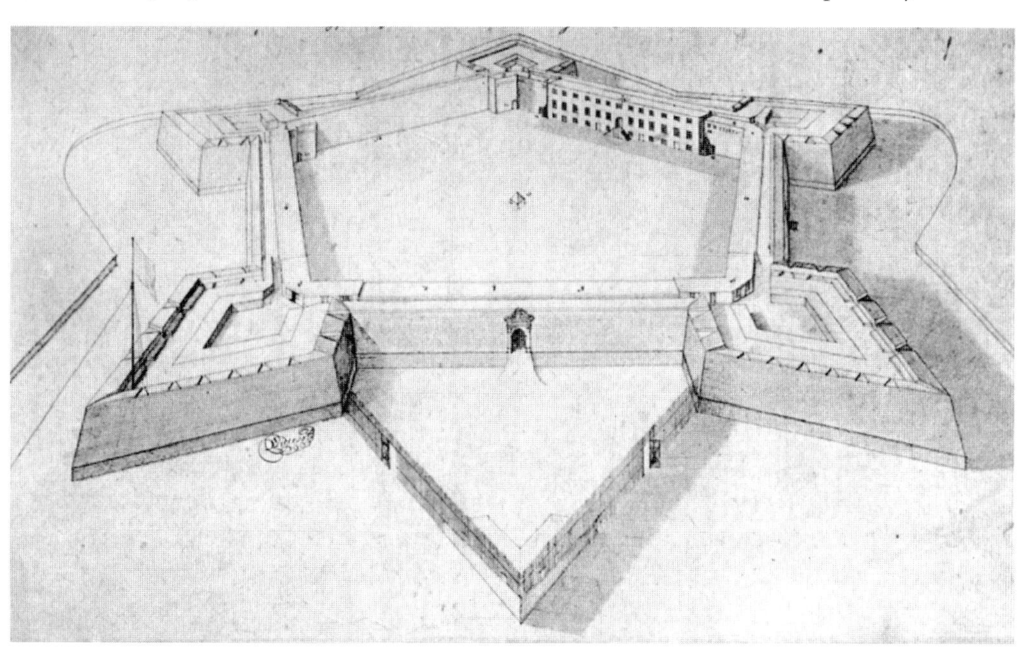

Sketch of the new stone castle that replaced the old mud fort. The bastions were named in honour of Prince William III: Buren, Nassau, Catzenellenbogen, Oranje and Leerdam.

Company records show that the Commander and his wife owned several slaves, and one can safely assume that slave women and female Khoekhoe servants were also enlisted to labour on the castle.

To their credit, the Van Herenthals completed the building of the fifth bastion while they were in office. Aletta, however, did not have long to make her mark at the Cape. In 1678 Johan died of pneumonia. Most of her friends and relatives were in Batavia and Aletta returned there, where she outlived her husband by only two years. She did not take part in the naming of the five bastions of the completed castle, which took place in 1679.

Cornelia Six: a shadowy figure

Amongst the entourage of Simon van der Stel, who arrived at the Cape in 1679, was Cornelia Six, Van der Stel's unmarried sister-in-law. Cornelia's older sister and Van der Stel's wife, Johanna Six, had flatly refused to come to the Cape with her husband and children. There is much conjecture as to her reasons. The most popular view is that her husband's bad-tempered, aggressive behaviour discouraged her, and that the thought of having to endure the trials of a primitive foreign country on top of an unhappy marriage simply proved too much. Van der Stel was also at loggerheads with his mother-in-law, who took Johanna's side.

The wife of the Commander of the Cape was expected to play a visible role as moral and social supporter during her husband's tenure of office, to smooth his path and leave him free to carry out Company business. Could an unmarried woman also make a valuable contribution to the tenure of a Commander? Considering the first two years of office of Simon van der Stel, with this unlikely shadowy female companion standing behind him, it seems possible.

Probably in her early thirties, Cornelia was not a flighty young girl looking for adventure. A document drawn up before her departure from the Netherlands describes her as a "bejerde dochter".[26] At the christening of Simon's fifth child, Henrico, in 1670, Cornelia signed as one of the witnesses, indicating that she was probably the child's godmother: she had a close relationship with the children and was aware of the responsibility of looking after them.

Cornelia Six must have attended many social functions with Van der Stel as his official hostess, but there is no record of any notable act that she performed. Single women had little status in society. She arrived at the Cape in 1679 and lived out her brief stay there in the shadow of her energetic and seemingly self-sufficient brother-in-law, choosing one of the traditional roles for women, that of foster mother to his six children.

But was Cornelia so unassuming? She was a woman of some mettle, standing firm against her mother and sister, and there is no doubt that Van der Stel saw her both as a reliable ally and a substitute mother for his children. She was probably fairly well informed about the Cape, as her uncle, Bax van Herenthals, had been the previous Commander. An aging spinster, Cornelia probably seized the opportunity to become the First Lady of the Cape. This enabled her to lead a full social life, mixing with more marriageable men than she would have met in the Netherlands. The Cape was a hunting ground for unmarried women, and Cornelia probably hoped to find a suitable husband there. Even if there were

26 Böeseken, *Jan van Riebeeck en sy Gesin*, p 28.

The letter-writer, painted in the studio of Gerard Ter Borch, before 1681, showing typical dress of a wealthy Cape lady.

few wealthy free burghers, many ambitious and socially well-placed young men and widowers stopped off on their way to Batavia or on the return trip to the Netherlands.

At the Cape, Cornelia's circumstances were a far cry from the luxury she was used to in the Netherlands. Although Cornelia had slaves and servants to help her mind her young charges, and was better dressed and fed than the majority of the woman pioneers at the Cape, the Van der Stel family's accommodation was abysmal. Granted, she did not have to camp in a tent or live in a leaking mud and wood fort, which had been the lot of Maria de la Queillerie, but the castle was in a rundown state. The Van der Stels were forced to take up residence in the house used by the previous Commander, Van Herenthals. The state of this house also left much to be desired; in fact, the VOC had ordered that the house be razed and that the new Commander reside in the castle.

Renovations started at the castle and the Van der Stels moved in in June 1680, but Cornelia did not have much time to enjoy the improved accommodation. Wealth and privilege were no guarantee of good health at the Cape. She died on 21 May 1681 after suffering for 12 days from a severe fever. She was buried under the floor of the Groote Kerk.

After Cornelia's death Van der Stel refused to undertake his usual journeys to the outlying areas, and confined himself to duties within the castle. It was only five months later that he could bring himself to ride to Stellenbosch, where the farmers were involved in a serious dispute over boundaries. Cornelia, the shadowy figure, the aging spinster and child minder, had been his mainstay, allowing him tackle his first years at the Cape.

Even in death, there were economic distinctions at the Cape. The rich were buried under the church floor, while the poor were relegated to plots outside the church, under what is now a public parking area. Unfortunately, when the Groote Kerk was rebuilt in 1830-40, Cornelia's grave and that of Simon van der Stel disappeared under the new building. If you stand with your back to the magnificently carved altar, facing the congregation, your left foot will be above Simon van der Stel's grave and your right foot will be over Ryk Tulbagh, who governed the Cape from 1751 until his death in 1771. Six governors of the Cape are buried in a square within that area. Various members of upper society, such as Cornelia Six and wealthy landowner and Company official Olaf Bergh (Angela of Bengal's son-in-law) were buried under sections of the church floor. However, space was at a premium even for the rich, and by the time the church was rebuilt, the coffins of the rich were stacked one on top of the other, as many as six deep, under the floor of the old church.

CHAPTER 5

Enduring slavery

An abhorrent feature of the early Cape settlement was the presence of a large population of slaves, who were bought and sold by Huguenot, Dutch and German settlers as well as by Company officials.

In the 17th century, European colonists considered the use of slaves an absolute necessity; indeed, the colonial project may not have been possible without the use of slave labour, which was used to run the settlers' large farms and households and the Company grounds. However, the indigenous Khoekhoen were not at first amenable to working as servants or herdsmen for the settlers, and the VOC would not allow their enslavement.

One of the first official requests Jan van Riebeeck made, in May 1652, was for permission to purchase slaves to do heavy work, which included maintaining the provision gardens, building the fort, hauling wood and quarrying stone. This was work for men, but female slaves were also needed at the Dutch settlement.

Slaves, however, were an expensive commodity. Although the VOC, through its possessions in the East Indies, had ready access to the slave trade, it informed Van Riebeeck that it could not comply with his request immediately. It took another five years before the Company provided the settlement with

Slaves being captured in Guinea. There were a handful of West African slaves at the Cape. They were originally bound for the Americas on Portuguese slavers, when their ships were captured by the Dutch and their cargoes re-routed via the Cape to the East.

slave labour; after that the slave trade flourished at the Cape.

The slave trade

Dutch ships carrying cargoes to and from the East sailed into Table Bay, and slaves could be purchased from the captains. Apart from the East Indies, sources of slaves included Madagascar and Mozambique, both of which were on Arab slave-trading routes. A few West African slaves were also bought at the Cape. By 1700, it is estimated that 50% of the slaves at the Cape came from various parts of the coast of India; Bengali or a similar language was probably widely spoken.

African slaves were often imported in large groups from particular areas, especially Madagascar, Angola and Guinea. For them, there was at least a chance that some relatives and friends would be bought by neighbouring owners or even the same household. Sometimes relatives arrived later, as happened to a Malagasy interpreter who witnessed his aunt being sold at an auction a few months after he arrived at the Cape.

Conditions on slave ships were inhumane. Both male and female slaves were given meagre rations of food and water, barely enough to ensure survival. Fitted head to toe like sardines in a tin and normally lying down, the slaves were battened down into airless holds. The temperatures off the coast of Africa for most of the year were high and the heat and

Map showing the origins of the slaves brought to the Cape. Only a few slaves were from West Africa, the majority initially coming from East Africa and Madagascar. The term "Malay slaves" is inaccurate; slaves from the East came from a variety of countries, many of them from the coast of India.

humidity in those holds often caused death by suffocation. Even the crew of sailing ships, who were well fed in comparison to their slave cargo, often died of scurvy and contagious tropical diseases. Almost every entry in Jan van Riebeeck's journal that records the arrival of a ship in Table Bay lists the number who had died on the voyage and how many were still suffering from scurvy and fever. Apart from the physical miseries of the voyage, the psychological stress endured by slave men and women was immense and many must have suffered intense depression.

The first slaves at the Cape were indispensable to the economic wellbeing of the society. Zacharias Wagenaar, Van Riebeeck's replacement, had little trouble procuring slaves for the Cape because they had more than proved their worth. Indeed, there were more slaves at the Cape than in other contemporary slave-owning colonies.

Male slaves were more expensive, but females were far more versatile: most of the African slave women worked in the fields but could also be assigned to housework, cooking and babysitting if necessary. Women also produced children, who could be sold or employed in the running of the household or the farm.

Slave women were among the first workers in the vegetable gardens and vineyards at the Cape. From the first sale of African female slaves in 1658, 22 were assigned to work in the Company's gardens. As free burghers began to move inland, more female slaves became workers in the vineyards and grain lands of the western and south-western Cape. Slave women were also the essential support system of individual households and government institutions. Having slaves to serve as cooks, housemaids, wet nurses, nursemaids, washerwomen and seamstresses, many settler women were freed of the mundane, time-consuming and often dirty tasks of the household. This meant that the mistress could devote time to social pursuits such as entertaining and supporting her husband's career. For farmers' wives there was more time to produce butter, cheese, preserves and handcrafts.

Furthermore, slaves were good business: the price of a slave escalated from the time of purchase – for example, Henricus Muncerus purchased Susanna of Bengal for the price of 65 rix dollars from Simon van der Stel and sold her two months later for 75 rixdollars. As the Cape settlement grew, buying and reselling became a thriving business.

A life of misery

Slavery benefited the settler community, but for the many slaves at the Cape it was a life of misery. Often children were sold separately to their mothers and married couples were parted; accommodation was normally rudimentary, with several slaves sharing cramped quarters; food was inadequate; and many owners meted out excessive physical punishment to their slaves.

Slave-owners made careful notes in their records of descent and place of origin. Not all slaves had surnames, depending on local customs. The practice of substituting the name of the respective country of origin tells us where they came from and who they were. Maria of Bengal, Catryn of Coromadel, Florinda of Nagapatam, Diana of Cochin, Anne of Batavia, Sara of Ceylon, Flora of Timor and Rebecca of Masutipatnam were all from the East. Women from Bali, Borneo, Java, Ambon, Japoer, Bougis and Cheribon were highly valued by slave-owners at the Cape.

Slave women of African origin included Mary of Guinea, Gloria and Helena of Madagascar, Elizabeth of Angola and Maria of Punta de Gale. The first names of these women were of course given to them by their Cape owners; their real names were not recorded.

Although slaves were not permitted to marry each other at the Cape, the Van Riebeeck household slaves and some of the Company slaves appear to have arrived at the fort as married couples or were allowed to cohabit as common-law couples. Their names are linked in the records, as in the case of Dirchie and Dirk of Guinea and the Angolan slave couples, Marselij and Mathija, Franscijn and Domingo, Mary and Thomas Keuben, Mary Pekenijn and Jan Meuw and Isobel and Ouwe Jan.

So strong was the love and loyalty between these couples that the Dutch used it as insurance against rebellion by the male slaves. When faced by a Khoekhoe attack in 1659, male slaves owned by the free burghers and the Company were armed with assegais to fight alongside their masters. Their female companions were locked up in the fort as hostages to ensure that the men supported the Dutch – it was believed that "they are apparently much attached to their womenfolk and would not readily desert them."[27] This proved to be true: no male slaves deserted on this occasion and they fought alongside their masters against the Khoekoen.

One of the biggest problems slave-owners at the Cape faced was desertion by both female and male slaves, who often left in pairs. By August 1658 the official figure for slave desertions stood at 28, of which about one third were women. In October 1658 a couple owned by free burgher Steven Janssen fled inland after stealing a pistol and clothes worth 40 guilders from their master. No doubt they planned to join other runaway slaves.

Harsh punishments did not deter slaves from escaping. Many of them sought refuge with local Khoekhoe clans, but in 1658 the Dutch threatened the Khoekhoen with war for harbouring these refugees. The Khoekhoen denied everything, but mysteriously several slaves, both men and women, were back on their masters' properties within a few days. Most of them seemed bewildered and unhappy. A single female slave was found in a bemused state next to the mill on her masters' property, where she had apparently spent the night out in the open. Another woman and her male companion stood forlornly at their masters' farmhouse door in the middle of the night, waiting for someone to acknowledge their presence.

At first these runaways were all locked up in the fort as punishment, but their owners, mostly free burghers, requested that a meeting be held with the Company officials to take a decision about their punishment so that the slaves could return to work without delay. Regardless of their sex, all the returned slaves were tied to poles in a public place and brutally whipped. One of them was branded too, and two others chained together. By decree of the fort, chaining slaves together to prevent escape was one of the few punishments not normally inflicted on females, young children, the sick and the aged.

One of the first attempts to westernise both African and Eastern slaves at the Cape was the institution of a few hours of daily schooling in the Dutch language and the Christian

27 Thom, *Journal of Jan van Riebeeck*, vol III, p 52.

Eastern slaves being sold at a dock in the Netherlands – C T Thompson.

religion. Those who complied were offered a reward of some tobacco and a tot of brandy. Although the Dutch in theory wanted their slaves to be baptised as Christians, in practice this was not always desirable, because this would entitle the slave to freedom. (They were not always given freedom, though). Statistics of manumissions in the 17th century are incomplete, but records indicate that although 331 slaves were baptised from 1665 to 1695, only 100 manumissions occurred. In fact, many manumitted slaves were not baptised and conversely many of those enslaved were baptised, church-going Christians.) A large section of the slave-owning population also did not encourage their slaves to become Christians, feeling that Christianity was for white people.

Despite these hardships and deprivations, many slaves managed to endure, and in some cases rise above the ignominy of slavery. Among the slave women were some extraordinary personalities who left their mark on Cape history.

Islam in the slave community

Although at first Christianity attracted many slaves, a large section of the slave population refused to give up their religion: Islam. This proved to be one of the biggest obstacles to conversion to Christianity. Islam also drew

Eastern slaves who were not originally of the Muslim faith, and many African slaves as well. It was the religion of the oppressed, and conversion to Islam was an act of defiance against the Europeans, who tried to own the slaves body and soul.

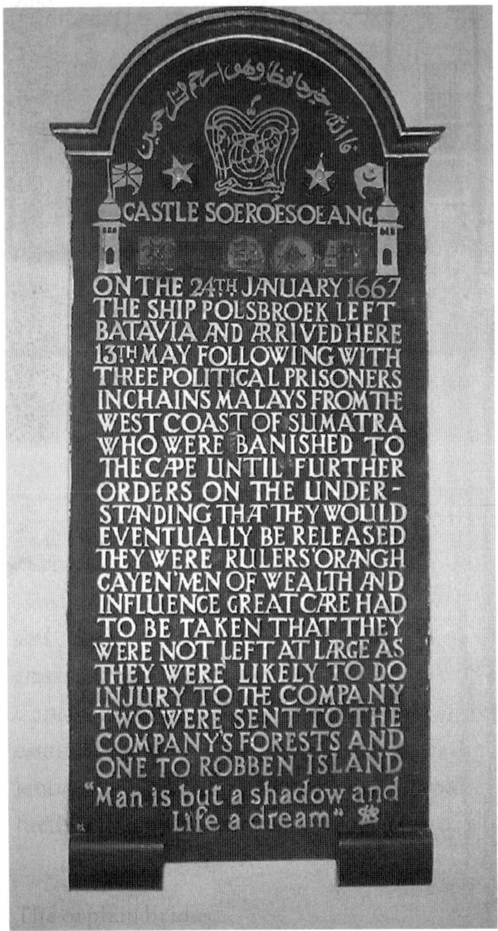

A plaque in the tomb of Sayed Mahmud, in Summit Road, Constantia. Kramats, the holy shrines of Islam, mark the graves of Muslim Holy Men. There are more than 20 recognised kramats in the Peninsula area, with at least another three in the outlying districts of Faure, Caledon, Rawsonville and Bain's Kloof. Both Sayed Mahmud and Sheikh Abdurahman Matebe Shah arrived at the Cape in 1667, and their tombs are the oldest known kramats in South Africa.

One of the first communities to spread the faith of Islam in the Cape was the entourage of the Shaykh Yusuf, a political exile from Goa. He arrived in 1694 with a retinue of 49 people, which included his wives Carecontoe and Carenone, two slave girls, Mu'minah and Na'imah, and 12 children. The government at the Cape decided on the farm of Zandvliet near Faure as a residence for the exiled group. The reasoning was that the farm was not close enough to the Cape settlement for any political or religious agitation to take place amongst any local supporters. The farm became a refuge for fugitive slaves and a meeting place for other political exiles from the East. Nonetheless, the Company's policy of holding Yusuf captive in an isolated area ensured that the spread of Islam was "contained".

The Dutch were so determined to stamp out the spread of Islam that from 1652 until 1795, slave owners who "suffered slaves to embrace the tenets of Mohammedanism"[28] were punished by severe fines or confiscation of their slaves. Yet these measures failed to stop the spread of Islam, which flourished at the Cape.

Eva from Madagascar

There were 11 slaves working in and around the fort by the beginning of 1658, eight of whom were women. Most were stowaways or had been given to Van Riebeeck as gifts. The first two slaves acquired in this fashion were men and the third was Eva, a 30-year-old African woman from Madagascar. Frederick Verburgh, a Company employee, brought her to the Cape on 12 December 1654 as a gift

28 Shell, "From Rites to Rebellion", p 11.

The tomb of Sheikh Abdurahman Matebe Shah at the entrance to Klein Constantia. Sheikh Abdurahman was the last of the Malaccan Sultans, whose ancestors established the first Malaysian Empire.

for Van Riebeeck, along with her young son, Jan Bruyn. Eva can perhaps be counted amongst the lucky ones: at least she survived the hellish sea journey to the Cape.

Eva performed none of the duties assigned to her at the fort satisfactorily. The Van Riebeeck family accused her of being lazy and could not persuade her to obey their orders. The only apparent solution was to send her away to Robben Island as a shepherdess. On 29 May 1657 she boarded the *Robbejacht* in Table Bay and set sail, making history as the first woman to be banished to the island.

Ever since Van Riebeeck stocked Robben Island in 1653, sheep had thrived there. The island was free from predators and there was good grazing. To counter theft by passing sailors, four or five shepherds were stationed on the island. A shed was built to serve as living quarters and a vegetable garden was started.

Conditions on Robben Island were grim. It was arid, windswept and lonely. Two white convicts and a black stowaway from the mainland shared Eva's banishment. Part of this quartet's punishment was a strictly rationed food supply from the Company. The other inhabitants were male stonecutters working on the island, who received meat or bacon and a tot of brandy every day, while the four miscreants were condemned to catch birds on the island if they wanted any meat and were only allowed a tot of brandy every second day.

Herding sheep on the island was hard and dangerous work and Eva was not content. Jan Woutersen, the postholder (superintendent) on the island, complained about "Eva who does nothing but run about the island, chasing the sheep and driving them from their lambs. She needs someone to look after her and does not heed and cannot understand signs, gestures or thrashings, so that no credit can be gained at this work with such people."[29] Indeed, most of those who ended up working on the island neglected their duties, or their work did not come up to expectations. Jan Woutersen himself allowed so many sheep and rabbits to die that the Company officials felt that Eva was a more successful shepherdess, despite Woutersen's continual complaints about her. Worse still, he failed to keep the beacons going day and night, causing danger to ships entering Table Bay through the treacherous waters around the island.

Eva's behaviour was probably a form of defiance. The Dutch had separated her from her small son, whom she had left behind at the fort. The first time she saw him again was on 28 March 1658, when she was in charge of 20 sheep that were being delivered to the fort, but this was a brief visit. The Dutch authorities decided that she must return to Robben Island to take up her duties again, and on the 30 July 1658 she sailed back on the *Schapenjacht* to her bleak and lonely prison. The midwinter seas were huge and rough. The captain reported that his passenger "was so sea sick that we thought she was dead, but she recovered completely when the sea calmed down".[30] Her condition improved once she stepped off the ship, but her attitude towards her herding duties did not.

Eva had little comprehension of the Dutch language and no inclination to learn it. She must have been extremely lonely: at the time she was the only permanent female resident on Robben Island. Her companions could not speak her language and presumably the Dutch did not encourage her to have much social contact with the men. Rebellious and unwilling to even try to learn the language of her hated captors, Eva was obviously at a disadvantage and severely unhappy. Even beatings failed to control her behaviour.

Worse punishment followed when Eva was subsequently shipped off to Batavia with a shipload of Angolan slaves – apparently by mistake. Tragically, her son did not travel with her. There are no records of who owned him thereafter or even whether he reached adulthood. Jan Bruyn's name is not on the list of slaves Van Riebeeck sold when he left the Cape, nor is it in any of the Company's records.

Two years after Eva had left the island, in 1659, the Company lost almost its entire flock of sheep when they tumbled down a ravine in wet wintry weather. The supervisor on the island at the time remarked that it was a miracle that the shepherds (male) had not been injured. No incident of this sort happened during Eva's two-year term as shepherdess: despite her unruly behaviour, she had proved her worth.

The nameless beacon-keeper

Rough and manual work, like Eva's duties, was usually assigned to African slaves. Inside homes, the lighter duties of cook, personal maid, nursemaid or seamstress were usually given to female slaves of Asian origin. Thus there were more black slaves on Robben Island, where the work was considered too heavy for Asian women.

In January 1659, a female slave was assigned

29 Thom, *Journal of Jan van Riebeeck*, vol III, p 133.
30 Thom, *Journal of Jan van Riebeeck*, vol II, p 321.

with her common-law husband to take over Woutersen's work of maintaining the beacons on Robben Island. The couple were to chop wood, carry it to the signal beacon and keep the beacon alight day and night. This key commission required a person of impressive character. The woman's husband was ordered to help his wife with the heaviest work, but she was the one to take responsibility for the task. An entry dated the 24th January 1659 in the Van Riebeeck's Journal states that "instead of another Dutchman we send you the female slave you requested. She is most hard-working and you can use her, together with the slave who is already there who is regarded as her husband, to chop wood and carry it to the beacon hill."[31]

From time to time other slave women were sent to Robben Island for short periods for various duties, such as cutting twigs and bushes to fuel the beacon, weeding out thornbushes from the grazing areas, gathering suitable bedding for the sheep shed and collecting and loading sea shells onto the boats for transportation back to the fort.

Caterina: the first freed slave

Besides being an important part of the labour force, slave women filled another vacuum at the Cape: they provided marriage partners for settler men. Men, both settlers and slaves, far outnumbered women. However, despite the shortage of marriageable females, from 1656 to 1669 only three marriages between slave women and white men took place – all three brides being of Eastern origin.

For some lucky women, marriage to a white man was a route to freedom, as well as a step up in society, even if the burgher was poor. Many of the slave matriarchs were loved companions and wives of husbands who relied upon them for help in running farms and businesses as well as rearing large families.

In 1656 Caterina, daughter of Anthonie of Bengal, married Jan Woutersen, a Company employee. Her former owner, the Admiral Bogaert, liberated her when she requested permission to get married, asking no money in return. Caterina made history as the first liberated slave in the Cape and the first to be classified as a "free black", a term applied to all freed slaves, whatever their colour or creed. Upon manumission, Caterina's official description in the record books changed from female slave to the "Honourable young daughter Catharina Anthonis".

Jan was appointed superintendent of Robben Island, but as previously mentioned, he failed woefully in his duties and was demoted in 1658 to the rank of soldier. The family was ordered to leave the Cape. The stay on Robben Island could not have been pleasant for Caterina. She was pregnant and gave birth to her child there – probably the first person born on the island. With her husband and child she left for India in March 1658 on board the *Schelvis.* Although they departed in disgrace, Caterina left as a free woman and her destination, while not her homeland, was at least a more familiar culture than the one she had found at the Cape.

Angela of Bengal: the matriarch

To a slave woman conversion to Christianity and marriage to a white man was a double bonus: she gained her freedom, and was launched into a more desirable position in society. There were, however, drawbacks. Women of mixed or slave descent, despite

31 Thom, *Journal of Jan van Riebeeck*, vol. III, pp 5-6.

their new-found status as married women, were often shunned by their white counterparts. There were of course exceptions to the rule – women who "enjoyed the advantages and made full use of them".[32] Angela of Bengal was just such a remarkable woman. She built up a respectable reputation at the Cape and certainly contributed towards both its labour force and later its agricultural economy.

When Company officials at the Cape were transferred to the East or back to the Netherlands, some were humane and set their slaves free before departure, while others sold them off to another master. Jan van Riebeeck chose the latter option, selling off all his slaves well in advance before leaving for Batavia.

Angela of Bengal was one of the women, along with Christijn of Angola, sold by Van Riebeeck to Abraham Gabbema, the Company fiscal. Fortunately for these women, Gabbema also purchased Angela's three children as well as Christijn's small daughter, Mary. This was not the common practice: owners generally treated slaves as if they had no family feelings or need for parental love. If a child was old enough to perform any useful duties it was considered saleable and quite often separated from its family.

Angela was obviously a good servant in the Gabbema household. When he was transferred to Batavia in 1666, Gabbema freed Angela and her three children. What is puzzling is the disappearance of Angela's husband from the records; there is no mention made of him when she is sold. The death and birth of slaves was often poorly documented.

After manumission, many slaves had to fend for themselves, but Gabbema made provision for the welfare of Angela and her children for at least six months thereafter. An arrangement was made with Thomas Muller to provide the little family with lodging, food and clothes in return for Angela keeping house for him. If after six months Angela wished to stay on in this capacity, Muller would be obliged to pay her a salary.

Freedom to Angela was the green light for a productive and successful life. At the end of her six-month employment period with Muller, she chose to leave and try to support herself. Free blacks were allowed to purchase land, and in February 1667 she bought a property adjoining the Heerengracht. Her neighbours were the most eminent free burghers in the town.

Financially she coped extremely well and even had the funds in March 1668 to hire an African male slave, Scipio Malabar, for the sum of five guilders per month. We do not know how she managed so well; possibly she started a small market garden and sold the produce to ships in Table Bay.

Socially she became a well-respected member of the settler community and a pillar of the local Dutch Reformed Church, where she was baptised on the 29 April 1668. Conversion to Christianity elevated her social standing with her Dutch neighbours. A few months after her own baptism she brought her son Pieter to be baptised and thereafter stood as godmother to two infants, both of slave descent. Marriage to a respected free burgher and wealthy farmer, Arnoldus Willemsz, increased Angela's social standing in the community. They were married for 20 years, and she bore him seven children. During his marriage to Angela he reverted to the family name of Basson. Angela Basson neè Bengal was therefore the matriarch of the vast Basson family in South Africa.

32 Shell, *Children of Bondage*, pp 327-328

Angela was a matriarch of whom the family can be proud. When her husband died in 1689 he left her his estate of 6 495 guilders. She owned farmland, and at the time of her death in 1720 her heirs inherited several well cared-for properties and farms. She also left them the sum of 14 808.30 guilders, which she had accumulated by judicious management of the proceeds of her husband's estate. Her estate was divided between her daughter, Anna de Koning, born of Angela's first marriage or liaison with slave Domingo de Koning, her granddaughter, Catherina van de Sande and her grandson, Arnoldus Maasdorp.

Angela of Bengal had successfully integrated herself and her family into the upper social stratum of the Cape settlers and taken full advantage of all it had to offer.

Anna married the explorer and captain of the Company garrison, Oloff Bergh, who brought back samples of copper from Namaqualand at the time of Simon van der Stel's governorship of the Cape. Although in 1668 Company officials were forbidden to own land, Anna's husband was among several men who disregarded this regulation, profiting from illegal land grabs. After Simon van der Stel's death his huge Con-

A portrait of Anna de Koning, daughter of Angela of Bengal, who later married explorer Oloff Bergh.

stantia estate was divided into three parts for sale: Bergvliet, De Hoop op Constantia and Constantia. Bergh bought Constantia. Anna was the mother of ten children whom she brought up on the farm. When Oloff died she farmed alone for ten years before selling the property. She was also the owner of several other prosperous farms. Descendants of Anna Bergh married into the Louw family, and part of this vast family bears Angela's genes.

When Maria de la Quellerie's granddaughter, Johanna Maria, visited the Cape in 1710 she met Angela of Bengal. In a letter to her parents dated 16 March 1710 she describes Angela as "Ansiela . . . the old black woman" who was "married to a Hollander B . . ." and whose daughter was married to Captain Bergh. Ansiela told Johanna that she had worked for her parents as a nursemaid to her mother, aunts and uncle, and that she cherished fond memories of the Van Riebeeck household. Johanna also visited a "black woman" named "Swarte Maria". Her mother, Mary of Guinea, had been a slave in Jan van Riebeeck's household and had been a nursemaid to Johanna's father. Maria gave Johanna a packet of seeds as a present for her father, Abraham van Riebeeck.[33]

Larger than life: Groot Catrijn

Not all slave women led exemplary lives like Angela of Bengal's. Angela's life-long friend, Groot Catrijn of Palicacatta, was a colourful character. She was a Company slave to Van Riebeeck and several other officials.

In 1667, gambling was illegal. Given the dearth of entertainment, however, it was an illicit pastime enjoyed by all strata of society. Two young officers at the fort organised an evening's gambling with Catrijn. She played enthusiastically, despite the fact that she was losing heavily to the two young men. At the end of the game she owed them 80 rix dollars, which she promptly paid. Foolishly, they boasted of their ill-gained booty and were summoned to appear before the Council of Justice. Catrijn was also required to appear and give evidence about the evening's gambling. The Council warned all three that if they were caught gambling again their punishment would be severe. The men were sentenced to pay 25 rix dollars each to Catrijn as well as a fine to the court. As army officers in responsible positions and earning a reliable income, they had, in the court's view, taken unfair advantage of Catrijn. She was not made to pay a fine to the Court, and her only loss was the balance of 30 rix dollars she had already paid the officers.

This incident gives an interesting perspective on the control exercised over female Company slaves' free time, as well as the high value placed on these women. Evidently there was frequent social contact with male officials, which was not frowned upon as long as the men were not sexually involved with the slave women. The officers who had erred were reprimanded not for fraternising with a female slave, but for gambling.

However, illicit romances with slave women were not sanctioned by the Company. Gossip circulated about the affair between Mary of Bengal and a constable in charge of the armoury, Willem Cornelius. In a cloak-and-dagger plot on the night of 22 August 1660, at midnight, three witnesses burst into the constable's room and found the couple. The ill-fated lovers were promptly separated, but Mary received the better part of the bargain. She was locked up,

33 Bosman, *Briewe van Johanna Maria van Riebeeck*, pp 88, 104.

confined to her room in the slave quarters and warned about her behaviour. Her lover faced far harsher punishment. He was dismissed from his post and sentenced to pay a fine of 50 reals[34] for immoral behaviour.

On 20 December 1671, Catrijn married a free black, Anthonij of Bengal. Christoffel Snyman is recorded as the child of this marriage, but he was in fact fathered by Hans Christoffel Snyman, a soldier at the fort. In the case of Mary of Bengal, who was found in the bed of her white lover, as well as that of Catrijn, who was similarly caught with Snyman, it was the men who received the punishment and not the women. Both female slaves were acquitted with a warning about loose morals. It would appear that in some legal cases, being a woman and a slave acted as some form of protection from harsh punishment.

Catrijn realised the worth of a Christian baptism: she was baptised in 1668 and had her son Christoffel baptised in 1689. Her fellow slave and friend, Angela of Bengal, stood as witness at Catrijn's baptism and as godmother to Catrijn's son.

Christoffel Snyman was the progenitor of the Snyman family in South Africa. He later married Marguerite de Savoye, daughter of one of the wealthier French Huguenot families. The marriage was unique, as it is one of only two recorded marriages between white women and ex-slaves of mixed origin.

Maria Everts: a prosperous landowner

Between 1660 and 1705 more marriages occurred between white men and freed slave women. Although Asian women were still popular, Cape-born women of mixed parentage made up the majority of these brides, and there were also a few recorded marriages to African slave women. Most appear to have been manumitted before their marriage. These women were accepted into society if they were baptised Christians. Elizabeth of Makinas, a black slave who married Coenraad Buys, followed the typical pattern of ensuring her children's future by having all of them baptised.

Although undoubtedly racial prejudice existed, especially towards mixed marriages, white society was often prepared to set aside issues of class and race if enough money and land were involved. A prominent family who owned De Hoop of Constantia was descended from an African female slave, Anna of Guinea. After she and her husband, Evert of Guinea, were freed they bought land in Table Bay. Their daughter, Maria Everts, married a penniless white man, Bastiaan Colyn. (Despite the fact that Maria's first marriage to Jackie Joy, a slave from Angola, had not been dissolved.) At the time of her marriage to Colyn, Maria was a prosperous landowner in possession of a wine farm planted with 400 vines. The work on the farm was done by three slaves, all owned by Maria.

The liaison was a profitable one and in 1709 Maria was able to buy more slaves: two women, seven men and a young boy. At the same time she also employed a white foreman for the farming activities and to supervise the slaves. At the end of that year Maria was the owner of 24 cows, 300 sheep and 6 000 vines; the farm produced wine and corn for sale. In contrast to his wife's wealth, Colyn's listed possessions in 1707 amounted only to a pistol, a gun and a dagger: all the material wealth of the farm remained firmly in her own hands.

34 Reals were coins minted by the VOC specifically for use in trade with the East. They were issued to sailors in its employ sailing to the East. The real was widely circulated in the Netherlands and therefore acceptable currency at the Cape settlement.

Maria's slave background was overlooked because of her wealth and ability to run a profitable farm. Both Maria's children married well and were accepted into the landowning white society. But wealthy free blacks like Angela of Bengal and Maria Everts were the exceptions to the rule. There was little hope for most slave women, either Company or privately owned, of ever gaining their freedom, let alone owning land. Conversion to Christianity, being set free by a compassionate owner or marriage to a free man were the only escape routes, and open to few.

Lijsbeth van de Caap: passion, hate and a stormy affair

Many of the freed female slaves married or lived with freed male slaves. Marriage normally took place between freed slaves from similar backgrounds and places of origin. In marriages of this kind, the descendants usually became part of the free black community.

The relationship of Lijsbeth van de Caap and Anthonie of Bengal was as dramatic as any. On 27 July 1663 Anthonie, a freed slave and landowner, bought the freedom of Lijsbeth and two of her children. The condition of her manumission was that she continued to keep house for him and serve him faithfully for several more years. Although the fathers of most of Lijsbeth's children are unknown, it is likely that Anthonie fathered the two manumitted children. For the next four years the couple lived together, and apparently it was a happy arrangement. On 17 March 1687 they appeared before the magistrate and made a promise to get married.

Less than a year later the partners had not set a wedding date and were at loggerheads. After a particularly fierce argument, Lijsbeth left Anthonie to stay at her mother's house, asking to be released from her betrothal. She said that one of the reasons for the breakup of the relationship was that Anthonie abused her, hitting her and threatening to kill her. Matters were so bad that she sought a restraining order from the magistrate. Anthonie claimed that he had every right to punish her because Lijsbeth had been unfaithful to him with his shepherd. In revenge he sacked William Teerling, an Englishman, and claimed compensation of 475 guilders from him for stealing not only the affection of Lijsbeth but also some of his sheep.

The worst punishment he saved for his ex-lover. He applied to the court for her re-enslavement on the grounds that she was not a baptised Christian and therefore did not deserve the honour of manumission. Another vindictive stab was Anthonie's claim for custody of the youngest child. Lamentably the court granted the latter request, on the condition that Anthonie pay the child's mother all costs incurred in raising the child to that date. However, the magistrate refused to have Lijsbeth re-enslaved and also ruled that Anthonie had no further right punish her in any way. She and Teerling set up home together. Anthonie was quick to get over his hurt feelings; he married another freed slave, Rebecca of Macassar, on 24 March 1694.

The tragedy of slave children

A great deal of a female slave's value to her owner was the fact that she could procreate. The children she bore automatically became the property of the owner. In Roman Dutch law, which applied at the Cape, children took the status of their mother – thus a slave woman's children were automatically slaves.

A portrait of Captain Hendrik Storm and his children on the roof of their Cape Town house. While this painting dates from 1760, it illustrates the relationship between slaves and slave-owners that was established in the 17th century. Note the barefoot slaves in the background.

In 1685, Baron van Reede tot Drakestein, a commissioner sent to inspect the work of Simon van der Stel at the Cape, visited the Company slave lodge and was horrified at the number of slave children with European blood. He urged Van der Stel to encourage white free burghers and Company officials to marry these slave women – but at a price. The groom had to recompense the Company for the loss of its property, calculated at about 150 guilders. Those who could not afford to pay had to sign a contract that entitled the Company to half the man's estate, should his slave wife die before he had paid off the bride price. An attempt was made to prevent more children of mixed parentage being born in the Lodge, and a law was passed that white men were not allowed to take slave concubines, with heavy penalties. However, this law does not appear to have had much effect; three quarters of the children born to slave mothers in the Company slave lodge had white fathers.

Many more children were born to slave mothers owned by free burghers. There was no law preventing private owners from forcing their slaves into prostitution. A profitable sideline for a slave-owner was to hire a female slave out to a bachelor as his concubine. This not only relieved the owner of buying food and clothing, but also earned them a tidy sum every month. If a child was borne by the "courtesan slave", the father had to pay for its food, clothing, housing and education, but ultimately the child of this union still belonged to the original slave-owner, who could sell the child if he wished.

Such children became so valuable that some slave girls reported that their madams forced them to sleep with any willing white man, in the hopes that they would become pregnant. One timid and unwilling young girl complained that although she resisted fiercely, her mistress threw her into the bedroom of a male visitor, locked the door and removed the key.

Many slave women probably became concubines of white men in the hopes of a marriage proposal, but these were few and far between. Their only consolation was that their children stood a better chance of entering into white society, which held the key to economic and social advancement.

Saddest of all was the plight of small children torn from their parents, reared in strange households and brought up as slaves. Maria de la Quellerie, Van Riebeeck's wife, owned three small girls. "Klein Eva" (to distinguish her from Eva of Madagascar) was a present from the "King of Antonjie". She had been brought to the Cape by the same Frederick Verburgh who delivered the hapless older Eva. The child was only five years old when she arrived at the fort. The other two children came from Abyssinia (now Ethiopia), and the Slave Register describes them as Arab girls. Lijsbeth was ten years old and Cornelia was 12. All three of the little girls, Klein Eva, Lijsbeth and Cornelia, were lent to Company officials with the understanding that one day they would be legally returned to the Van Riebeeck family. Lijsbeth and Cornelia went to work for Verburgh's widow, Maria. Both were converted to Christianity and baptised.

Occasionally a slave family was lucky and a buyer would purchase the entire family. Van Riebeeck bought Angela of Bengal, her husband and her three children as a family from Commander Peter Kemp, and later sold Angela and the children to the fiscal, Gabbema.

In 1666 Thomas Muller, in whose household Angela of Bengal worked as a temporary housekeeper, bought an African slave woman, Gugeima of Guinea, for 100 rix dollars. Gugeima had an eight-year-old daughter, Mary. According to Company law, if the child of a slave was not fed or clothed by the Company, the parent was allowed to buy the child's freedom. Doubtless some officials ignored this law or found a way to prevent the loss of a profitable future slave. Fortunately for Gugeima, Muller was an honourable man; when he purchased her in 1688, he promised that he would set her daughter free – and so he did, on 19 January 1672.

Two VOC commissioners to the Cape (Goske in 1671 and Baron van Reede in 1685) declared that children with European fathers should be manumitted; this became policy in 1688 but it was never enforced. Marriage to a burgher, however, meant that a slave woman might have the means to buy the freedom of her children – who would still legally be the possessions of her former owner. If a slave woman married an ex-slave, she was not automatically freed, but he was allowed to buy the freedom of his wife and children. For both men and women this process sometimes took years of scrimping and saving and backbreaking toil. Most women who married settlers married poor men, and those who were married to freed slaves, or received their freedom as a single mother, normally had little money.

The many children of extramarital unions

between slave women and white burghers were sometimes accepted by white society, and their children often married white people. This was the case in the Odendaal family. Their stammoeder was Susanna Biebouw. She was born in 1667 of an extramarital relationship between her mother, Diana van de Kaap, who was a slave, and settler Detlef Biebouw. Her father acknowledged her as his daughter and she was accepted into the white community. She married a burgher, Willem Odendaal, in 1711.

The Classen (or Claasen) family, a common "white" surname in South Africa, has several slave forebears. The first of the Classens to form a liaison with a slave woman was Cornelis Classen from Holland. Catryn of Bengal bore him several children, including a son, Claas, born in 1673, and a daughter, Alida, who was christened in 1685. In turn, these children and other members of the Classen family married people of mixed origin. Johannes Classen, another progenitor of the Classen family in South Africa, came to the Cape from the Netherlands in the early 1700s, and married Johanna de Rek, whose mother was a slave, Constantia of Bengal; Johanna's father was probably white. Johannes's father is named as Claas of Malabar, and his mother was probably of mixed origin. This generation of Classens were all socially acceptable in the white community.

The pitiful case of Susanna Een Oor

By 1668, all female Company slaves were housed in one large room of the slave lodge, together with their small children. Susanna of Bengal's baby girl cried continuously. There was no milk for the child because Susanna was ill and her milk had dried up; none of the other slave women offered to suckle the child. From the records it appears that Susanna was ostracised by the other women. Her nickname was "Susanna Een Oor" and she was a convict who had been banished to the Cape. (Criminals of both sexes were often branded by the lopping off of one ear.)

When the time came to extinguish the candles in the lodge, Susanna's child was still wailing pitifully and, according to her testimony, Susanna was afraid that the other women would be annoyed. In desperation she pressed some rags over the child's mouth to keep it quiet.

The testimony of the other women differed from Susanna's. They maintained that she attempted to strangle her child with a length of rope under cover of darkness. If this version is true, she probably hoped that people would assume that she had smothered the child in her sleep by lying on it, not an uncommon occurrence.

Babies born in the slave lodge were a valuable commodity – they were a future work force for whom no purchase price had to be paid. (Indeed, in 1665 a cash incentive was given to Company slave women to bear children, but as fertility rates increased the reward was discontinued.)To the Company, infanticide meant the loss of a valuable future slave. Rewards were offered to slave women to report any such occurrences.

The slave women were not prepared to let unpopular Susanna's baby die. Several of them overwhelmed her, a struggle ensued and they managed to pull the baby from her grasp. But their efforts to save the child's life were in vain. Eight days later it died in agony. The verdict of the Company surgeon after the postmortem was that the baby died of a ruptured gall bladder. This could have been caused by Susanna's manhandling the baby in her attempt to strangle it – but no one pointed out that the damage could have been done to the child in the struggle between the women, nor the fact that a diseased gall bladder could have been the reason why the child had been crying so. None of the women appeared to be remorseful about not offering to suckle the sick and hungry baby.

What complicates the evidence even more is the fact that the Court disallowed Susanna's first testimony, and then had her tortured with thumbscrews. Only after this painful ordeal did she change her version of the story and confess to attempted murder.

Susanna was found guilty of murdering her baby. The original sentence was to have her breasts gouged off by hot irons, and then for her to be burnt alive until her body was reduced to ashes. The sentence was commuted to a punishment felt to be more humane. On 13 December 1669 she was condemned to be sewn alive into a sack, dropped into the deep waters of Table Bay and left to drown.

This was a tragic end to a life that appears to have been filled with unhappiness. The sad fact of Susanna's story is that her child would probably not have survived adulthood, as the death rate for both infants and adults in the slave lodge was very high, due to long working hours and atrocious living conditions.

The hell of the slave lodge

In 1679, in keeping with the expansion of Company projects, the VOC built a new slave lodge to house its many slaves; this brick building was a breeding ground of filth and disease. Both infant and adult mortality for the inhabitants was high, and few survived into their thirties.

The Slave Lodge as it is today. The lodge, at the corner of Wale and Adderley streets in central Cape Town, is now a public monument and a museum of cultural history.

Slaves lived in cramped, overcrowded, unsanitary conditions. Men, women, children – slaves alongside convicts – all slept, ate and spent what little spare time they had in one room. At one stage, pigs wandered though the courtyard. If the Company hospital was full, patients from passing ships were bedded in the slave lodge, no doubt adding more germs to the already contaminated air.

In 1685 Baron van Reede castigated Simon van der Stel about his ill-treatment of the Company slaves. In the bitter cold and rain of winter, women worked for long hours in the fields and gardens, some with babies tied on their backs. Their clothes were in tatters and many garments appeared not to be Company issue, but hand-me-downs from passing sailors.

Although there was a law forbidding sexual intercourse between slaves and white men, the Company turned a blind eye to this. Slave women at the lodge earned those second-hand clothes, and some comforts like tobacco, alcohol, or money, by turning to prostitution. Some slave women did not choose prostitution, but were forced to sleep with white men by their own common-law slave husbands, who acted as pimps.

The VOC, with its vast trading network and the huge numbers of sailors, soldiers, officials, traders and travellers visiting its outposts, had a natural link with prostitution, which flourished in the great ports of the Netherlands and the East. One of the results was the birth of many children of mixed parentage at the slave lodge. In fact it was to the Company's benefit to encourage prostitution at the lodge, as any children born were owned by the Company.

At the time of Baron van Reede's visit to the Cape, slave children had no schooling. Slaves at the slave lodge had no access to churches, which was in keeping with the reluctance of the Company to free baptised Christian slaves. This was anathema to Van Reede, who attempted to institute some improvements, one of which was that a female teacher be employed to teach the girls. However, a male teacher, Jan Pasquel, was employed for both boys and girls – and was eventully banished to Mauritius because he sexually abused his pupils.

Sadly, few other improvements were made. One of these was the appointment in 1688 of binnemoeders ("inside mothers") in the slave lodge. The binnemoeders were chosen from the ranks of the slave women living within the lodge. Their most important duties included supervising the making of soup for the slaves, and nursing in the hospital. If a child was very ill, a slave mother was supposed to be excused from work on that day in order to be with her child. In practice this did not apply. A record of a day in 1710 shows that there were 19 sick children in the hospital, but only one mother was allowed off work.

White women were appointed as "outside mothers" to supervise girls under 14 years of age by teaching them good manners and handicrafts, such as the art of embroidery and the making of clothes from wool and linen. To encourage this labour, the girls were allowed to charge for their services and to keep the money. However, they did not make much profit as most of their labour was in the service of their mistresses, who had first call on their talents. Any pocket money they earned was strictly monitored by the binnemoeders, who allowed them to spend their hard-earned money only on material or clothes. The style and colours they chose had to be approved by the binnemoeders. In effect, this practice saved the Company from buying clothes for the slave girls.

Armosyn van die Kaap and her daughters

Armosyn Claar van die Kaap, born in about 1661, was a slave of either Guinean or Angolan ancestry. She raised three daughters in the filth and misery of the slave lodge, but her descendants found freedom. Armosyn tried to ensure the future of her children by having them baptised in the Christian church.

One of her daughters, by an unknown father, was Manda Gratia. Manda was born and brought up in the slave lodge, and eventually rose to become one of the matrons of the lodge. She must have been a woman of considerable strength of character: matron was the highest position a female slave could aspire to. The slave lodge as a whole was under the eye of a male slave supervisor, a mandoor, but the matron, with the assistance of an under-mistress, supervised the female slave section. Both these posts were coveted, as the women who held them received small amounts of cash for their services, and the matron had her own room away from the crowding of the communual female quarters. Even here there were barriers: not any slave could aspire to those positions – only mixed-race women were suitable in the eyes of the Company officials.

Four children from different fathers were born to Manda during her stay at the lodge; all of them were slaves. One of the children was a daughter, Margaretha Gertruy. When Manda married one Frisnet in 1714 he adopted the girl, bought her freedom and legally gave her his surname. It is assumed therefore that Margaretha was Frisnet's daughter. He did not, however, buy the freedom of Manda's three sons, and by the time the time of her death a few years later in 1719, Manda had only succeeded in buying the freedom of her youngest son, Frans Lewen.

Armosyn had two other daughters who were also born at the lodge and who started life as Company slaves: Maria Stuart Cleef – who died at sea, still in the service of the Company – and Magdalena Ley. The third daughter of Armosyn and her union with an unknown white man, Magadalena Ley was another member of Armoysn's line who obtained her freedom by marrying a white burgher, Hermanus Combrink. The Combrink family was accepted by Cape white society and Magdalena's son, Jan, married a white woman, Maria Magdalena van Deventer. One of Maria Stuart's daughters, Maria Francina Cleef, was freed and eventually married a soldier and "kneg", Heinrich Peter Hesse, in 1731.

The Town House, Greenmarket Square, in 1764.

CHAPTER 6

Working women

In the 17th century, the VOC was the biggest company in the world, offering a wide range of employment opportunities to soldiers, sailors, farmers, artisans, tradesmen, clerks, ministers, and many others. Men desperate to make a living – unemployed or so badly paid that they were willing to risk the unknown – flocked from all over Europe to

Detail from *Interior of a peasant dwelling*, a 17th-century painting by David Teniers the Younger. Women at the Cape cooked with a variety of home-grown fruit and vegetables.

seek employment with the Company. The VOC took advantage of the situation, and most of its employees were poorly paid.

These fortune-seekers hoped that moving to the Cape would bring them employment, enrich them and enable them to become landowners. But the majority of the first pioneers at the Cape lived from hand to mouth on non-productive smallholdings, or were soldiers or sailors whose contracts were temporary and pay uncertain. Company employees absconded regularly from their posts and attempted to stow away on ships bound for Holland.

The women who came to the Cape were also largely from poor backgrounds. Most were working-class women trying to make their way in the world – garrison wives, labourers and farmers. Some were in desperate financial straits and willing to turn their hand to any venture to survive.

These women were not strangers to hard work: in their home towns in the Netherlands, women helped to lay the cobbled streets, used their scrubbing brushes to keep marketplaces spotlessly clean, and many could sail a boat with ease. Dutch and German woman pioneers who grew up on farms were accustomed to manual labour: hoisting bales of hay and carrying heavy milk pails over their shoulders or on their heads. To the Cape they brought their practical knowledge, experience and determination.

The first free burghers

In 1652, when the VOC dispatched Van Riebeeck's party to the Cape, the Company was not interested in colonising the area. Its aim was purely commercial: to establish a refreshment station and harbour for the benefit of trade to and from the East. Nonetheless, it was imperative for the success of the Cape refreshment station to get as much land as possible under cultivation to supplement the fresh produce from the Company gardens.

A few Company employees were allowed to start small market gardens near the fort and sell their produce to passing ships, but this did not meet the growing need for fresh produce. In 1656, Van Riebeeck applied to the VOC for permission to release VOC employees who wished to farm from their contract with the Company, and thus become "free burghers". He also suggested that the VOC encourage Dutch farmers and their families to settle at the Cape.

In 1657, the VOC granted Van Riebeeck's request, and freehold land along the banks of the Liesbeeck River was given to nine free burghers – partly to as an incentive for people to settle in this lonely spot with its dearth of creature comforts and the constant threat of attacks from wild animals and the Khoekhoen. The free burghers were allocated land in the hopes that they would supplement the shortfall in Company provisions for the refreshment station as well as become self-supporting. The contribution of the hard-working farmers' wives was crucial to the success of these early farming ventures.

To protect these farmers and the Cape settlement, a series of small forts were erected along the Liesbeeck River and a huge hedge of wild almonds was grown to keep out the Khoekhoe raiders and the wild animals. The free burghers had little capital and, while they could now lease or own land, they remained heavily in debt to the Company, from whom they bought equipment, seeds and slaves on credit. They were only allowed to sell their goods to passing ships after the Company goods had been sold, and the Company fixed the prices. Most of the first free burghers had little experience in agriculture. Bad farming methods, droughts, animal diseases, and crop failure left them struggling to eke out a living.

After 1657, the Company decided to lease cattle to certain free burghers. One of the reasons for this policy was that "for the sake of the profit involved in this farming out system some tenants (especially the married ones) could be all the more easily induced to remain here instead of yearning to go on to India, as they do at present because of the poor prospects".[35]

By 1659, more men had left the Company's employ to become free burghers. "Town burghers" were those who lived in the area near the fort and the Company gardens, where they built houses. A few farmhouses also dotted the slopes of Table Mountain and Lion's Head. The town burghers and their wives were permitted to engage in market gardening from their small plots. In those early years there was no paid employment for women, and so the establishment of a small market garden gave women a much-needed opportunity to bolster the family income.

However, when the VOC granted permission to the town burghers to sell their produce to ships in Table Bay, something the free burghers in the Liesbeeck Valley were already doing, they had to abide by Company policies. A percentage of their produce had to be sold to the Company and only the surplus could then be sold to ships – and then only three days after the Company had sold its goods.

A housewife's life

Today when visiting the oldest farmhouses at the Cape, the visitor is greeted by large, airy rooms and impressive gables – architecture that signifies wealthy landowners; but this was not the case in the early days. The first houses were simple dwellings consisting of three rooms: a kitchen, a voorkamer (living room) and a bedroom. The roofs were sloped and thatched with local bulrushes and reeds, and the walls were constructed from clay or rubble. In later years, sun-baked bricks were used and covered by a layer of plaster and lime wash. The windows had no glass: instead they were covered with linen steeped in beeswax or whale oil. Local timber, usually yellowwood or wood from silver trees, was used for building.

By 1672, as the economy improved and more settlers came to the Cape, the original long three-roomed houses were extended into L-shapes by adding a kitchen onto the back of the house. Those whose fortunes were on the upswing built on another wing and the house became U-shaped, with a central courtyard. Some free burghers built their homes in a T-shape, allowing access from the central voorkamer to all rooms: bedrooms or a dining room were built on either side of the voorkamer, and the kitchen and any additional rooms were added on behind.

The first woman settlers lived under the communal roof of the fort where all the cooking was done by four Company-employed cooks. A free-burgher woman might have her own kitchen where she would cook for her family, usually assisted by a slave. The drawback was that this kitchen was not always well stocked. Until the gardens were well established and the stocks of cattle, sheep and goats were built up, the early Dutch pioneers were often at the point of starvation. They depended largely on supplies brought out from Holland aboard ships on their way to the

35 Thom, *Journal of Jan van Riebeeck*, vol I, p 347.

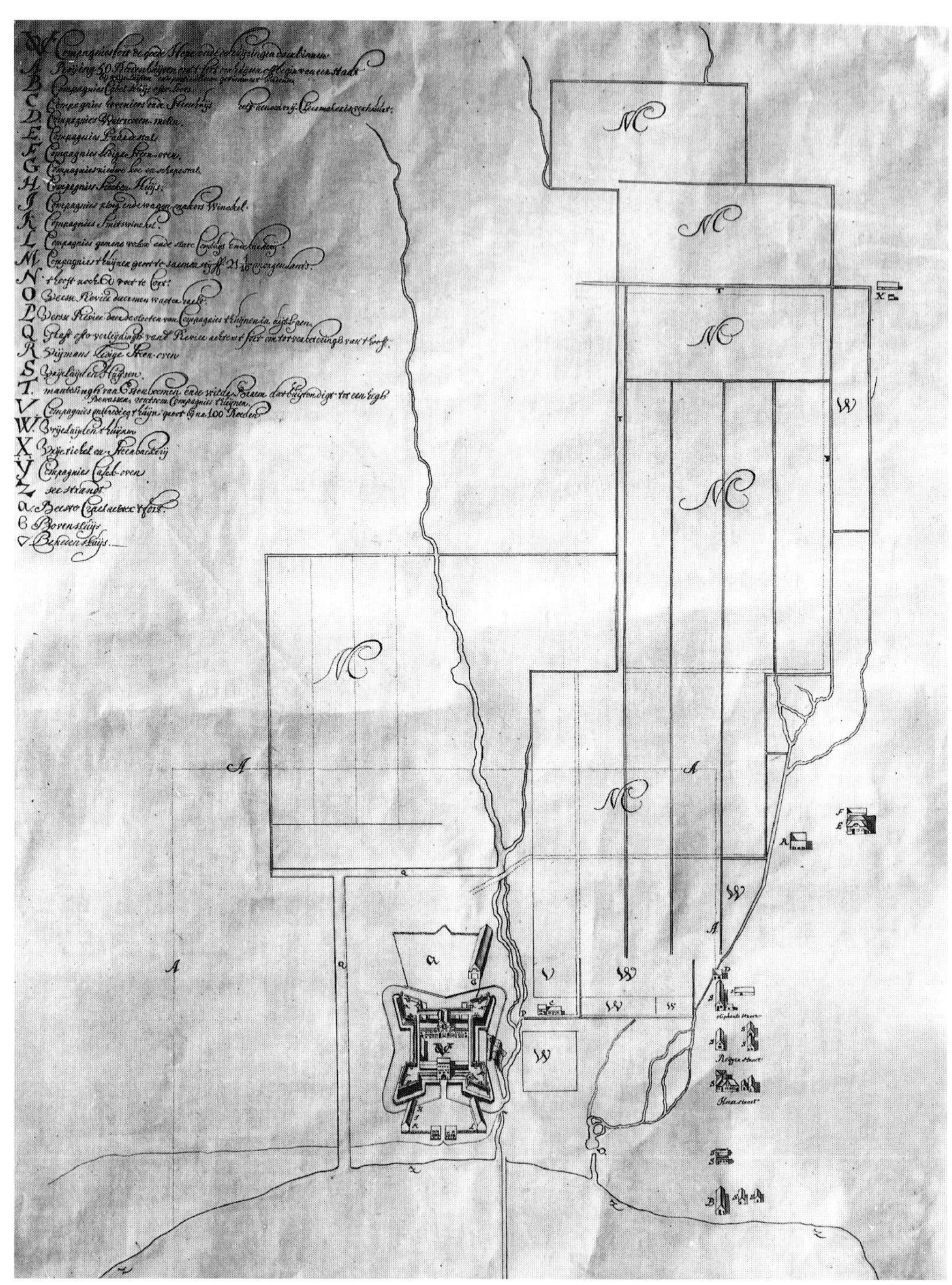

Plan of the settlement in 1660. Marked on the map are: A – boundary line; B – Company's cable-shed; C – gardener's house, let to a tailor; D – water mill; G – cowshed and sheepfold; H – hospital; I – shop for repairing ploughs and wagons; K – smithy; L – kitchen for common people and slaves; N – pier; O – river; Q – canal; R – brick-kiln; S – free burgher's houses (on Oliphant, Reyger and Heere Streets); V – Company gardens; W – gardens of the free burghers; a – cattle-pen; b, c – upper and lower sluice.

East. Conditions in the autumn of 1654 were so bad that in desperation Van Riebeeck sent a small boat to Saldanha Bay to collect penguin eggs and fish, and another boat to St Helena to ask a Company vessel for rice.

Resourceful cooks learnt about indigenous medicinal and edible plants from their Khoekhoe woman servants. Wild mustard and asparagus picked in the nearby veld were transplanted and thrived in the Company gardens. By 1657, when the first land was granted to the free burghers, a housewife could stock her kitchen with a large variety of fresh food. Peas, lettuces, endives, chervil, cauliflowers, red and white cabbages, beetroot, radishes, turnips, pumpkins, cucumbers, artichokes, watermelons, spanspek, horseradish as well as several varieties of beans and pulses were all available. In addition to supplies from the Company gardens, the authorities encouraged the housewife to cultivate her own small vegetable garden.

Typical dress of working-class Dutch women in the 17th century. A Khoehoe servant is in the background. Working women's dresses were made of cheap, hard-wearing material in bright colours, under which they wore colourful petticoats. Dresses were made so that they could be hitched up above the petticoats, to prevent soiling when doing dirty work. Scarves and bonnets made of cheap linen shielded them from the rain and the sun. A serviceable dark-coloured apron was worn daily, while white aprons were reserved for Sundays.

However, even with the variety of vegetables and fruit grown at the Cape, food was often in short supply because crops failed, were attacked by insects or wiped out by harsh weather.

Edible grapes took to the Cape soil, but although wine-making began in February 1659, wine production remained of such poor quality that Abraham van Riebeeck, Jan and Maria's son, on a visit to the Cape in 1676, commented that it still tasted like the liquid used to clean the vats. Hops for beer-brewing thrived and the first Cape brandy appeared in 1657. On the other hand, the Cape suffered from a scarcity of non-alcoholic drinks. There was no coffee and very little tea could be purchased, which meant that wine, spirits and beer were consumed at almost every meal – occasionally even at breakfast.

Bread remained a luxury for many years. During the first few years of the settlement, the population relied on dried bread or biscuits brought from the Netherlands to be sold at the Cape. Only with the granting of land to the first free burghers did the grain industry flourish and bread production begin. From 1657 onwards, the housewife had a choice of rye, oats, mielies, barley, groats and buckwheat to use for baking. Rice still came from Holland and Batavia, and potatoes were successfully cultivated at the Cape only at the end of the 17th century.

The seas around the Cape offered such a plentiful supply of fish and shellfish that seafood became a staple dish. For variety, penguins, penguin eggs and seagulls appeared regularly on the menu.

As far as red meat was concerned, this commodity remained in short supply in the early years of the settlement. While there was abundant game around the fort and the free burghers' farms, it seldom appeared on the table. The clumsy firearms available to the settlers made shooting game very difficult. (This was in marked contrast to the diet of the Khoekhoen, who were expert in trapping game and killing it with arrows and assegais.) Game in the pot for the family's supper was a rare treat for the pioneer Dutch. Dassies were the easiest wild animals to kill. Jan van Riebeeck wrote that their meat tasted more delicious than lamb and that when cooked they resembled six-week-old suckling pigs.

Another popular red meat was pork: live pigs were brought from Holland for breeding. They made a useful addition to sheep and cows, and supplemented the cattle and domestic stock bartered from the Khoekhoen. However, the Company found that while sheep and cattle prospered at the Cape, pigs died. This was put down to the herdsmen being so overworked that the pigs were neglected. The Company subsequently decided to sell the pigs, but only married free men could buy them – an indication of the value placed on the wife's contribution to the running of a successful farm.

For the farmer's wife, life was a constant battle to find enough food to keep her family from daily hunger, let alone stave off disease. By 1664, the plight of many of the free burghers was so bad that the local Company Council of Policy used the proceeds of Sunday church collections and fines to aid the stricken colonists, who were "burdened with naked children and through simple poverty must sleep each night beside livestock in the stable on a little straw and barren earth".[36]

36 Van der Merwe, *The Migrant Farmer*, p 5.

An artist's impression of Annetjie Boom and her family working in the Company gardens.

Annetjie Boom: she turned her hand to everything

Annetjie Boom was a member of the original Van Riebeeck party, with her husband Hendrik and their six small children. As head gardener, Hendrik's job was to maintain a steady supply of fresh fruit and vegetables for passing ships. The Booms were the first couple to be granted a piece of land adjoining the fort, within the area of the Company gardens. There they built their own house.

When the Khoekhoen threatened to attack in 1654, the Boom family home was in direct line of the planned onslaught. For Annetjie, sheltering in the fort when the Khoekhoen threatened to attack became a regular occurrence. In later years, when the Company began to grant more land adjoining the fort to an increasing number of free burghers, Dutch women and children were often forced to flee their homes to seek shelter in the enlarged fort.

The first Dutch women were no strangers to war – many of them or their families had experienced the Eighty Years' War (1568-1648) – and were adept at defending themselves. For example, on 17 June 1659, the wife of Jan de Wacht and Sophia Raderootjies, the wife of Jacob Cloete, became aware of an imminent Khoekhoe attack. They rushed out to warn their husbands, who were herding cattle, and when the attack began both women grabbed guns and took part in the fighting.

By 1655, despite the fact that Hendrik Boom held an important post, his pay did not cover his family's expenses. He successfully applied to the Commander for permission to lease some Company cattle. The duty of looking after the cattle fell to Annetjie, an experienced farmer, who had worked on a cattle farm in Holland – indeed, the lease was only granted to the Booms because of Annetjie's expertise. According to the contract, the Booms had to supply cheese, milk, butter and buttermilk to the Company for consumption at the fort, and also for sale to passing ships. Annetjie was granted the contract before the first free burghers were given land on which to farm, and thus could claim to be the first European dairy farmer in South Africa. (The Booms at the time were not free burghers, as Hendrik was still in the employ of the VOC.)

So successful was Annetjie's first period of cattle farming that when Hendrik applied in May 1656 for a bigger lease, this time for the entire Company herd, the Company granted it to him until January 1657. The Company decided to use Annetjie's business as an experiment. Her success or failure would be a measure of how viable it would be to lease out company-owned land and cattle to employees running their own private business concerns. It is recorded that "Annetjie the boerin, wife of the Company gardener, is willing to take the risk and has agreed to pay 100 guilders for the lease, whatever the number of cows".[37]

But despite her competence and enterprise, Annetjie was still poor. The Cape was not a place to get rich quick – the VOC made sure of that. She was deeply in debt to the Company and subject to their stringent rules. Annetjie therefore had to turn to yet another source to put food on the table: "In view of her burden of having to supply eight children and that she cannot make ends meet on her husband's bond money alone, she has, at her earnest request and on the strength of her claim that she is practically a free woman, provisionally been allowed to keep a tavern for the purpose of providing men from passing ships with lodging and refreshments."[38]

Mother of a vast brood, supportive wife, cattle farmer and inn-keeper, Annetjie Boom was an outstanding early South African entrepreneur. On the strength of her achievements, the Company decided to grant other employees the right to live on land outside the fort and to start their own business enterprises.

It seems, however, that the Booms overreached their capabilities by stretching their resources too thin. When the time came for renewing the lease, Annetjie was refused a further term. The Company felt that with their involvement with the inn and with gardening, the Booms were far too busy to carry on looking after the Company's cattle. Instead, the VOC decided to sell all the cattle to Jan Reiniersz.

Shortly thereafter, on 10 October 1657, Annetjie's lifestyle changed once more when her husband was granted his request to become a free burgher. Annetjie and Hendrik went ahead and bought their own cattle. Nothing at the Cape was uncomplicated, and owning livestock made a settler a prime target for Khoekhoe attacks and cattle rustling. On 30 June 1659 one of her Khoekhoe herders, who was trying to protect the herd, died from Khoekhoe assegai wounds. Despite the threat of danger from the Khoekhoen, Annetjie and her husband were determined to build a future for their family and by August 1659 they owned a farm of their own.

37 Thom, *Journal of Jan van Riebeeck*, vol II, p. 35.

38 Thom, *ibid.*, p. 35.

Thirteen years after their arrival at the Cape, the Booms returned to the Netherlands. Despite all their hard work, the chances are that they left completely disillusioned. In 1660, three years before their departure, dissatisfaction with Company policy and conditions at the Cape reached such a peak that 20 Company servants, 18 free burghers and three convicts stowed away on the return fleet. Another 26 potential stowaways failed and were captured. It appears that by 1662 little had been done to remedy the situation. Jan van Riebeeck, then governor of Malacca, submitted a frank report to the Batavian authorities on conditions at the Cape, which caused them to remark that some deception was necessary to attract settlers: "To make the Cape appear more than what it is in reality is, experience has taught us to be more bragging."[39]

The boarding-house keeper: Janneken Boddijs

Many women gritted their teeth in the face of difficulties and stuck it out. Following Annetjie's example, Janneken Boddijs, whose husband Jan van Harwarden was employed as the sergeant at the fort, applied for permission in 1657 to start a boarding house. She planned to offer accommodation to the increasing number of travellers passing through the Cape. To provide extra income, Janneken also asked for permission to breed pigs and to grow carrots and other vegetables to feed them.

The entrepreneurial spirit was not encouraged at the Cape. The Company would not tolerate competition against its monopoly on supplying passing ships, and Janneken's requests were granted only on condition that the Van Harwardens used the meat and vegetables they produced only for domestic consumption or to feed their lodgers – not to sell. Furthermore, they were not allotted prime land within the Company gardens area, but land that the Company considered unsuitable for growing prime crops. Janneken nevertheless became one of the first successful bidders to purchase Company-owned pigs.

One reason for the granting of the Van Harwarden request was the valuable assistance that Janneken and her children gave in building the fort. As a reward for their services, Jan received a salary increase on 5 July 1657.

The original fort of wood and mud needed constant repair. It could not withstand the harsh Cape winter rains and a replacement of more durable stone had to be built. However, labour was in short supply: the male labourers often refused to work because they were hungry and overtired. Pleas to captains of passing Company ships to assign parties of sailors to help were routinely refused. It fell to Janneken to undertake this traditionally male work.

Settlement life with its stresses and strains at least prepared women for coping on their own. During her marriage to Van Harwarden, Janneken had to cope alone for several long periods when Jan went on cattle-trading expeditions to Khoekhoe strongholds in the interior. In fact, these dangerous expeditions were often raiding parties that rustled cattle from Khoekhoen who were unwilling to trade. On his last expedition in November 1658, Jan stayed away for so long that Janneken feared that his party had met with disaster, and asked the fort officials to send out a search party. The offical report appears unsympathetic to Janneken's fears, comment-

39 Leibrandt, *Precis of the Archives, Letters Received,* vol II, p. 211.

The Cape of Good Hope in 1700, showing the castle, the settlement and the

ing that "The wife of Jan van Haarwaarden (as is natural with women) was getting anxious for her husband who was expected to return by today."[40] Jan eventually returned safely from a successful trading trip.

Janneken's struggle to make ends meet reached a crisis point on 18 February 1659, when Jan died and she was left with five small children to support. This was the second time that Janneken had been widowed. After Jan's death, when mention was made in Company records of his steady rise in the ranks from corporal to ensign and thereafter his thriving career as a free burgher, credit was given to Janneken's qualities as a good wife. In the eyes of the Company, she had enabled his success and stability.

Janneken, now the sole supporter of her family, had to be a shrewd businesswoman. She kept account of what was owing to her and claimed it without hesitation. On 17 May 1659, when the debts against the estate of the late Pieter Cleij were recorded, Janneken claimed her due. She had advanced the sum of 6 guilders to the deceased, as well as 14

40 Thom, *Journal of Jan van Riebeeck*, vol II, p 369.

gallows beneath Signal Hill.

guilders and 8 stuivers for food and drink that he had consumed during his stay at her inn.

Industrious and reliable women like Janneken were in great demand, and, even though she was the mother of five children, she only remained a widow for three years. On 18 May 1662, the first bans for marriage between her and Jocum Blank of Lubeck were read. For her third husband she chose another ambitious and hardworking man: Jochum had arrived at the Cape in 1655 as a cadet on a ship and had risen to the responsible position of dispenser and keeper of the pay books at the fort. When the banns for marriage were called, he announced his intention of becoming a free burgher as soon as he married Janneken.

The husband seekers: Beatrice Weijman and Hester Weijers

For women the early Cape was a good place for finding husbands. For the majority of women at that time marriage was a vital goal in life, as there were few opportunities for a woman to earn her own living. Marriage for men was just as important. The early pioneer women were involved in the day-to-day management of huge farms; they were helpmates as well as wives, and the rewards for a married free burgher were far greater than those for a bachelor.

There was a shortage of European women at the Cape – in 1658 there were 80 men employed at the garrison and 51 male free burghers, but only 20 Dutch women and children – and a single woman was assured of finding a partner. Many women were widowed and married several times. This was partly because of the shortage of marriageable women, but there were also sound financial reasons for marrying a widow: on her husband's death, a widow inherited half the property or assets. (The other half went to the children.) An ambitious young man would therefore come into a ready-made fortune if he married a wealthy widow. This was a more viable means of enrichment than marriage to a spinster: in the Cape, most young girls were members of huge working-class or farming families, and what little land there was to be inherited went to the sons. Thus white women at the Cape held a uniquely powerful position – because of their scarcity, and because of the system that entitled them to half the estate.

The dire shortage of women at the Cape resulted in many hasty marriages. Suitable young women on their way to Batavia or the Netherlands were quickly snapped up. The brides were ready to seize any opportunity to improve their lot in life – including marriage to a virtual stranger. When her ship docked in Cape Town on its way to the East, 23-year-old Beatrice Weijman, who hailed from Utrecht, met 33-year-old Jan Pietersz Louw, a widower and a farmer in the Liesbeeck Valley. Louw already had an established farm, and for Beatrice this was a chance to elevate her status in one fell swoop: to become a "respectable" married woman and the wife of a landowning free burgher. The ship was due to sail within three days, so special permission was received for the couple's banns to be called on those three consecutive days and they were married on the fourth. The marriage endured and Beatrice became the mother of a vast brood of children and the matriarch of the Louw family in South Africa. One of her grandsons married the granddaughter of the exceptional slave woman, Angela of Bengal, who served in Maria van Riebeeck's household.

Hester Weijers, born in Liere, a town near Antwerp, arrived at the Cape as a servant to the wealthy merchant William Basting. He owned the ship *Prins Willem*, which plied a regular trade to the Cape. When first mentioned in the Company records, Hester is described as "a virtuous young woman"[41] – a fairly common phrase used to describe unmarried women. Wouter Cornelisz Mostert asked for permission to marry Hester in March 1658, and in July they were wedded. The marriage soon showed its value: the Company awarded the sole contract for running the mill to Mostert, on the grounds that he was a "good industrious man" who had married "an industrious woman who strives to get on".[42] Hester also added to the family's finances by raising pigs.

However, Hester's "virtue" was publicly questioned. Theuntje Borns spread the rumour that Hester had been no virgin at the time of her marriage. In fact, she accused her of having given birth to two children in the Netherlands, one of whom she had strangled and the other abandoned. However, Theuntje was well known for her propensity for scandal and exaggeration. Hester defended her honour by bringing a case of malicious slander before Lacus, the Fiscal – a close confidante of Hester's husband.

Theuntje was found guilty, tied to a pole on the balcony of the fort for an hour, made to make public apologies to all she had wronged and thereafter banished to arid little Dassen Island for six weeks.

Intrepid adventurers: Anna Rudolphus and Francintjie van Lint

Marriageable women at the Cape were in such short supply that men were prepared to marry women who defied the social code. Even Anna Rudolphus was accepted as a welcome addition to the settlement. This intrepid young woman disguised herself as a soldier and sailed from Grietziel to the Cape aboard the *Gecroonde Leeu* in 1659. If this was to find romance, it succeeded. On the day before Christmas in 1659 she asked permission to marry Gijsbert Aressen, a free burgher trading as a mason, who was resident at the Cape. Despite Anna's flouting of both the social code and maritime law,

41 Thom, *Journal of Jan van Riebeeck*, vol II, pp 293-294.

42 Thom, *ibid.*, p 313.

the Cape officials unhesitatingly gave their consent, as female settlers were so highly prized.

Francintjie van Lint emulated Anna's example in February 1674 when she arrived at the Cape on the ship the *Gecroonde Vrede,* also disguised as a soldier. It did not take too long before Francintjie received a proposal of marriage from a free burgher. Commander Goske granted their request for her to stay on at the settlement and the wedding soon took place. No further mention is made of her, so presumably she lived till a good age.

Anna's fate differed from that of Francintjie. Along with new settlers and trade, the passing ships brought disease. In the first week of January 1660 a ship put into Table Bay, the crew and passengers suffering from a virulent strain of dysentery. Soon more than half the settlement were stricken and a slave died. Next to succumb on 7 January 1660 was Anna, who had stepped onto the Cape shore only a few weeks earlier, one of the few healthy survivors of the trip from Holland. She died before the date set for her wedding. A lasting memorial to her is a play written by Dutch playwright A. Francken, *Sussanna Reynier*, which commemorates Anna's short but adventurous life.

The oldest profession: Barbara Geems and Tryntjie Verwey

Even in the early days of the Cape settlement there were women who made a living from prostitution; there was no lack of clients. As we have seen, a natural link existed between prostitution and the VOC, as the vast trading empire of the Company spawned a lucrative sex trade both in the Netherlands and in all its far-flung trading posts. Sailors, soldiers, Company officials and adventurers trooped off the boats after voyages of five months and more, starved of female company.

Local men at the Cape also paid for the services of prostitutes, there being a shortage of women at the Cape. For many destitute women, prostitution was one of the few avenues where a woman could earn good money. For a prostitute or brothel madam, it was a livelihood which enabled a woman to be in charge of her own working hours and rates.

Barbara Geems, from Amsterdam, was born in 1628 and died in about 1687-88. Her first husband, Jacob Huybrechtsz van Rosendael from Leiden, arrived at the Cape in 1660 to work as a master gardener. For Barbara the Cape certainly did not turn out to be the land of opportunity. In 1662, her husband died. At the time she was pregnant and had two small children to support. Barbara was destitute and it appears that she married again in desperation. Her second husband, Hendrick Reynst, a free burgher and a carpenter, was ten years her junior. He turned out to be indolent and unproductive: the Company declared him to be one of the two laziest free burghers at the Cape. Hendrick successfully applied for a Company post, but there was no improvement in his performance, and in 1666 the Company transferred him to Mauritius.

While he was away, Barbara opened a brothel. In 1666, the Company's drummer, Hendrik Courts from Deventer, admitted in court that he had visited the brothel run by "Barbertjie Geems". The court records of the case of drummer Courts describe her as a whore and a brothel keeper – she was not only the madam, but also available to clients. Courts testified that when Barbara's services were unavailable, she forced her slave to cater to the needs of clients – this poor woman had no say in the matter, and as a slave would probably not have received any payment. In her defence, Barbara denied practicing prostitution, and lodged a complaint that Courts had slept with her slave twice, despite her objections. The Court sentenced Courts to three years' banishment on Robben Island.

When Hendrick Reynst returned to the Cape, he once more failed to make a living and in 1669 applied to the Company again for a post. Barbara decided to supplement the family income in a more law-abiding manner. In 1670 she applied to the Company to open up shop as a general dealer. Permission was granted on the grounds that she was a hard-working and capable woman. In 1676, Reynst died and Barbara was again the sole bread-winner; this time she opened up a bakery, which she ran for many years.

Despite Barbara's unsavoury reputation, Company officials and the Church Council were prepared to allow her to take in four foster children. In the records she is described as an industrious and competent woman, fitted for the task. Quite probably, Barbara did not take care of the children from the goodness of her heart but for the monetary allowance awarded to her for the task. All four children were of mixed parentage, and perhaps no other white woman was prepared to take them in.

As discussed earlier, three of Barbara's charges were the children of Krotoa and Peter van Meerhof. The fourth was baby Flotilda, a Khoekhoe baby who had been rescued from being buried alive alongside her dead mother. (According to Khoekhoe custom, a mother who died in childbirth was buried with her living child – an orphan was a burden on the rest of the clan, especially when resources were scarce.) The Church Council gave Barbara custody of Flotilda, on the sole condition that she have her baptised as a Christian. In return she received money for support as well as a servant – Flotilda was to be indentured to her until she reached marriageable age. The baby, however, died three months later.

Tryntjie Theunisse Verwey, also known as Ganzevanger (goose-catcher), arrived at the Cape in 1668 with her husband Gysbert and three children. He died soon after the family settled at the Cape. Tryntjie was desperate to support her family and turned to prostitution. As a result of what was termed in the Company records "an illegal means of earning a living", she had several brushes with the officials at the castle, who finally decided that they would award her land to help her earn a more respectable living. This was part of a charitable scheme devised by the Company to allot land in the Tijgerberg area to widows. The Company issued a warning to these hardy women that their farms would be subject to constant attacks from the Khoekhoen. Leopards (or as the Dutch called them, "spotted tigers") roamed in this area, as did lions and elephants. (These dangerous conditions still prevailed in 1698, when more small loan farms were granted in the Tijgerberg area.)

Tryntjie's farm, Doodekraal, soon flourished and her aptitude for farming earned her the nickname "boerin". However, it was not all plain sailing. Indeed, at first the grant of the land must have seemed to Tryntjie a punishment for her misdeeds. One of Tryntjie's shepherds was accosted by a party of 12 Khoekhoe warriors, who stole a sheep and killed it. When the shepherd tried to stop them the warriors tied him up and assaulted him. They then proceeded to kill another 16

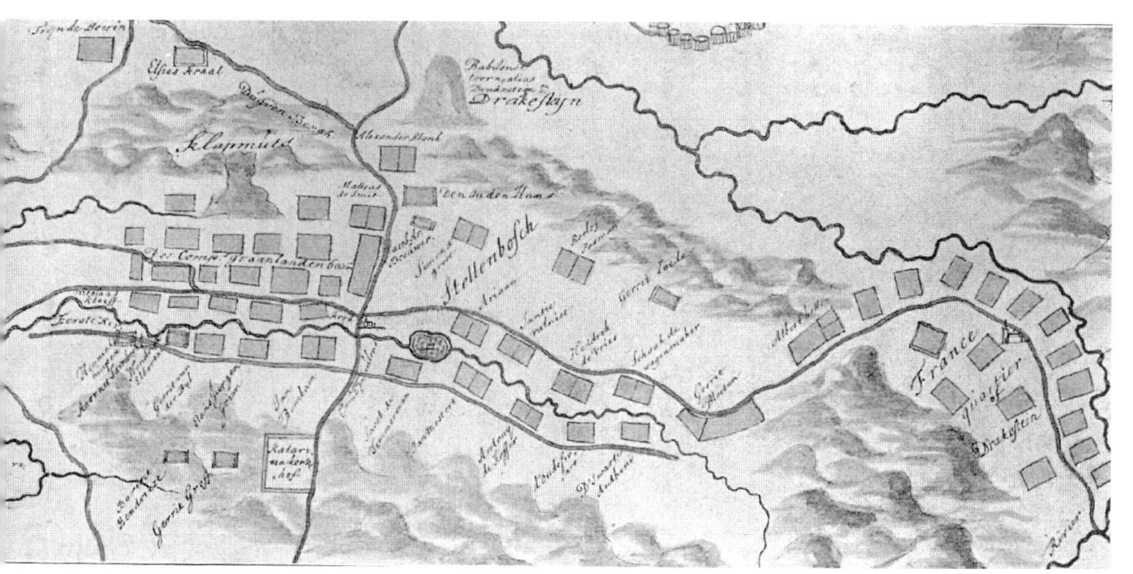

Part of a map of the settlement in around 1695. Trijn de Boerin's farm is indicated in the upper left corner.

sheep and had a merry feast, roasting the sheep over a fire. When they left, they drove the rest of the flock off with them. This loss was hard to bear for the impoverished Tryntjie.

But the VOC plan for self-supporting families bore fruit in the case of the Verwey daughters. Neither of Tryntjie's daughters turned to prostitution. Alida and Beatrix married the sons of a near neighbour, Hilletje Oliver, another widow who had been awarded land as a charity handout. Both daughters, like their mother, were widowed at an early age but managed to carry on running their farms.

In 1732, Beatrix Verwey was described as a widow "who has money"[43]; she was the owner of two freehold farms and one of the first farmers who could be called landed gentry, at a time when poverty and debt amongst farmers was rife. Beatrix was also amongst only eight individuals who were granted a grazing permit for land "in the dunes behind the grey hills".[44]

43 Guelke et al, *The De La Fontaine Report*, p 44.
44 Guelke & Shell, "An Early Landed Gentry", p 270.

Mayken Thielman Hendrickz and other "undesirables"

Many working-class women did not thrive at the Cape, sliding down the economic scale into dire poverty. Mayken Thielman Hendrickz was one such unfortunate woman.

The Company records in 1675 describe Mayken as a "poor and needy widow"[45]. She was forcibly removed from her home near the castle and in compensation granted a licence to brew "sugar beer". Mayken resorted to stealing rice and selling it. Mayken's punishment was severe: the Council took into consideration that during her marriage to Thielman Hendrickz, the couple had been fined on several occasions for illegal trading of livestock with the Khoekhoen, and that after her husband's death in 1673 she had twice been punished for stealing Khoekhoen cattle.

Accordingly, a rice sack was put over her head, she was flogged and branded, all her

45 Schoeman, *Armosyn van die Kaap*, p 494.

Morning gossip by Quiringh Gerritz Brekelenkam (before 1668) shows a typical working-class Cape interior.

property was confiscated and she was banished to Robben Island. However, her crimes were so heinous that the Company decided to rid themselves of this "poor and needy widow" for good and banished her to Mauritius.

A hardy survivor, Mayken created a new life on Mauritius. The last mention of her appears in the Company records of 1683, with a request to marry a Company gardener, Robert Hendricksz, and permission for them to become free burghers.

The boat transporting Mayken to Mauritius carried a boatload of "undesirable" and destitute persons for whom the Cape administration had no use. Mayken was the only one who was a branded thief. Other people on board included William Willemse, convicted of murder of a Khoekhoe, as well as his wife, Maria Visser, who committed adultery with the farm foreman, by whom she had two children during her husband's exile in Batavia. Theuntjie Borns, who had been banished to

Dassen Eiland for slandering the miller's wife, travelled to Mauritius for financial reasons: her husband Barthlomeus had failed to make a living at the Cape. Also on board ship were two of Krotoa's children, Pieternella and Salomon van Meerhof (her third child had died at the Cape), placed in the care of the struggling Borns family, to whom they were indentured as servants – orphans, like widows, were a burden to the Company. Daniel Zaijman, who would later marry Pieternella, was also on board; he had initially failed to make a living on Mauritius, then tried his hand at the Cape, and finally decided to return to the island. There were also six slaves on board, but they did not belong to any of the impoverished passengers: they were owned by the new administrator of Mauritius.

Expansion in the time of Van der Stel

As the 17th century wore on, it remained the policy of the VOC in the Netherlands not to encourage the creation of a colony at the Cape. The VOC was a private merchant company, not a Dutch governmental department, and its interests lay purely in profit.

The 17th century was the Golden Age of mercantilism for the Netherlands. Traffic in shipping to and from the East was heavy, and profits were good (although the Cape was making a loss). England and France cast covetous eyes on the rich Netherlands. In 1672 England and France signed the Dover Treaty, an alliance which planned to crush the Netherlands and seize all her possessions. Ijsbrand Goske, the Commander at the Cape at that time, was an exceptional military and maritime man, and concentrated on fortifying the castle and the coastline. During the war against the Netherlands, which ended in 1678, no English or French fleet threatened the Cape, but the Dutch were wary. The Commander who succeeded Goske, Van Heerenthals, continued fortifying the Cape on the VOC's instructions.

By 1679, even though the number of free burghers at the Cape had increased, only a small percentage were involved in agriculture. (Fewer than half were farmers; the majority were labourers, traders or skilled artisans.) Many were heavily in debt to the VOC, living on the breadline. The Cape settlement still had to import rice because it could not grow enough grain to feed its own population. However, despite being a constant drain on Company resources, the Cape was far too valuable a refreshment station to lose.

Although there was an ongoing policy of not promoting colonisation, the Company realised that one of the answers to making a profit at the Cape was the expansion of agriculture. More free burghers had to be encouraged to farm and a fresh batch of settlers had to be brought to the Cape.

In 1679 a new Commander arrived at the Cape, Simon van der Stel. He was faced with urgent problems. The population numbered 773 people, including free burghers, Company officials and slaves. However, only 22 families were self-sufficient. Though there were several thriving free burghers and farmers, many others were on the point of starvation. Van der Stel had strict instructions from the VOC to promote settler and agricultural expansion at the Cape to boost its flagging economy. To do this he had to encourage expansion into the interior, ensure the cultivation of more farmland, and spur more settlers on to become farmers. During his administration several changes were set in motion that affected every sector of the Cape population, especially hard-working farm women.

The burgher orphanage in Amsterdam. Ariaentjie Jacobs and her sister were among the group of eight orphans from this orphanage who volunteered to come to the Cape to marry free burghers. The girls at the orphanage wore a distinctive uniform, one side of which was red and the other black.

Van der Stel was enraptured with the beauty of the scenery surrounding an island in the Eerste River, as well as with the fertility of the soil. He decided that burghers must be encouraged to cultivate this land to alleviate the Cape's pressing food shortages. This led to the establishment of Van der Stel's Bosch (Stellenbosch), and the granting of more land further inland to intrepid free burghers.

The orphan brides

The ratio of women to men had not improved much by the time that Van der Stel became Commander of the Cape. He was concerned about the fact that male settlers far outnumbered women, and requested that 48 girls from Dutch orphanages be sent out to the Cape for the purpose of becoming hardworking wives. He promised that the orphans would be well provided for and were free to leave at once if they liked neither the Cape nor their future husbands. He also made a provision that, if after five years of marriage the young wives or their husbands wished to return to Europe, they would be free to leave at once.

Nonetheless, few orphans found the offer attractive. In 1685 only three girls decided to start a new life in Africa. Perhaps heartened by their example, the following year another eight embarked on married life at the Cape. They came from the largest orphanage in Rotterdam, which taught the girls to cook, sew, knit and carry out housekeeping duties, and wore a uniform that consisted of a red dress with a white apron.

True to his promise, Van der Stel saw to it that the girls were all married to thriving burghers. In some cases, the marriages were

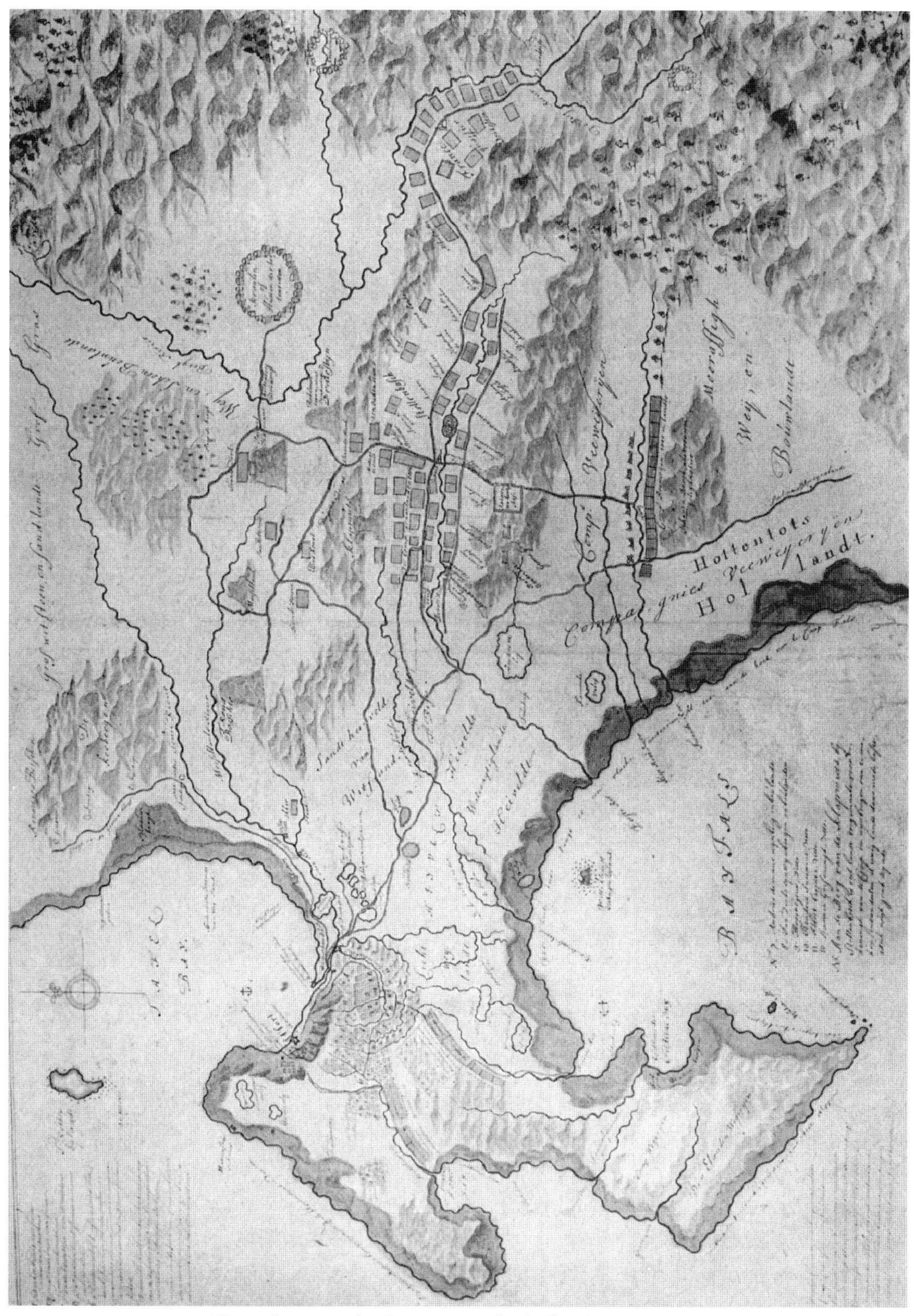

The settlement at the Cape c. 1695, clearly showing Cape Town, Stellenbosch and "France Quartier" (Drakenstein).

not successful: one orphan, Maria Swaanswijk, married the sick comforter of Stellenbosch, Sybrand Mankadan. Despite his duties as a lay preacher and moral leader in the community, his bride soon found out that Mankadan led a very unsavoury life. Van der Stel kept his word and there was a hasty divorce.

In the following years more orphans trickled out of Holland to marry Cape burghers, and several of them became matriarchs of well-known Afrikaans families. Ariaentjie Jacobs van den Berg and her sister Willemijntjie Ariens de Wit were in a party of eight orphan girls who landed at the Cape on 4 August 1688. Only 18 years old, Ariaentjie soon attracted an established burgher of Stellenbosch, Jan van Deventer, and married him on 29 October 1688. The speed of the marriage indicates that it was arranged; Van Deventer must have snapped her up as a prize (at the time there were 254 male free burghers at the Cape but only 88 married women and widows).

The Stellenbosch area had only been opened up in 1680; Ariaentjie moved into a young thriving community. Large families were the order of the day. This marriage produced eight children, making Ariaentjie the matriarch of the Van Deventer family in South Africa.

Ariaentjie and her sister have been identified as the carriers of the gene which causes porphyria – a disease that can cause urinary problems, skin rashes and bouts of dementia. (The madness of King George III of England is thought to be attributable to this disease.) One of Ariaentjie's granddaughters, Adriana van Deventer, married Johannes Colyn, son of the freed slave Maria Everts; another granddaughter, Maria Magdalena van Deventer, married Armosyn van die Kaap's grandson, Jan Hendrick Combrink.

CHAPTER 7

Catharina Ras

Cape society in the 17th Century has been called "one of the most polyglot populations in the world".[46] Besides the increasing number of slaves from Africa and the East, settlers from European countries continued to arrive at the Cape. The male population was very cosmopolitan: Dutch, Swedish, Norwegian, Flemish and German men all sought employment with the VOC.

While the majority of settler women at the Cape were Dutch, there were a few who hailed from other countries such as Germany. The small Dutch community appears to have welcomed the arrival of German women, who blended into the social and cultural environment with apparent ease.

The woman who lived through it all

One such German settler was Catharina Ufftincx (or Uistings), who arrived at the Cape in 1662, the week of Van Riebeeck's departure and the start of Wagenaar's administration. She died in 1706, and in the course of her life would have witnessed many changes at the Cape. Although the whole panorama of early European settler life cannot be gleaned from the life of one woman, the life of Catherina Uistings is fairly well documented in Company records; these accounts give a general background to life at the Cape at the time.

Catharina was tough and hardy, proving equal to the demands made on pioneering women. To have survived the nightmare voyage of five months from Texel to the Cape was a feat in itself. When her ship, the *Hof van Zeeland*, arrived on 25 July 1662, 20 people had died on board and 50 passengers and crew were dangerously ill from scurvy. After disembarkation there were many more deaths. Catharina appears to have been one of the few who arrived in good health.

She was adventurous and opportunistic. Born in Lubeck, this young woman was only 21 years old, widowed and alone when she arrived at the Cape, doubtless in search of a husband. This goal she speedily attained: on 2 September 1662 she married Hans Ras, a German settler. Hans had arrived at the Cape from Angelin in March 1658 as a mercenary. By 1660, he had left the employ of the VOC and become a free burgher and a farmer – he owned a house on the banks of the Liesbeeck River in Rondebosch, formerly the property of Jacob Cloete. It was to this property, on which stood a house and a barn, that Catharina came as a newly married woman.

If Catharina thought that she was marrying a wealthy man, she was wrong. Hans was amongst the men who attempted to stowaway in 1660 because of bad conditions at the Cape. The farm was not prospering and Hans could not afford to pay his servants. Whereas the Company officials all owned slaves, Hans complained that "he could not get any".[47]

The bride's wedding night was a fiasco. The guests and the newly married couple cele-

46 Shell, *Children of Bondage*, p xxv.

47 Worden et al, *Cape Town: the making of a city*, p 26.

brated after the wedding, and in an inebriated state climbed onto the two wagons that would take them back to Rondebosch. A race ensued. The wagons collided and one wagon left the road, causing Thielman Hendrickz, one of the drivers, to swear venomously. Hans Ras, infuriated that his bride and guests were subjected to such crude language on his wedding day, leapt from the bridal wagon and ordered Hendrickz to stop his offensive behaviour. Hendrickz's wife, Mayken, pulled Hans's hair while her husband knifed the bridegroom twice: the blade broke in half and stuck in his ribs. (As we read in the previous chapter, Mayken was later banished to Mauritius.) Catharina almost lost her new husband, but

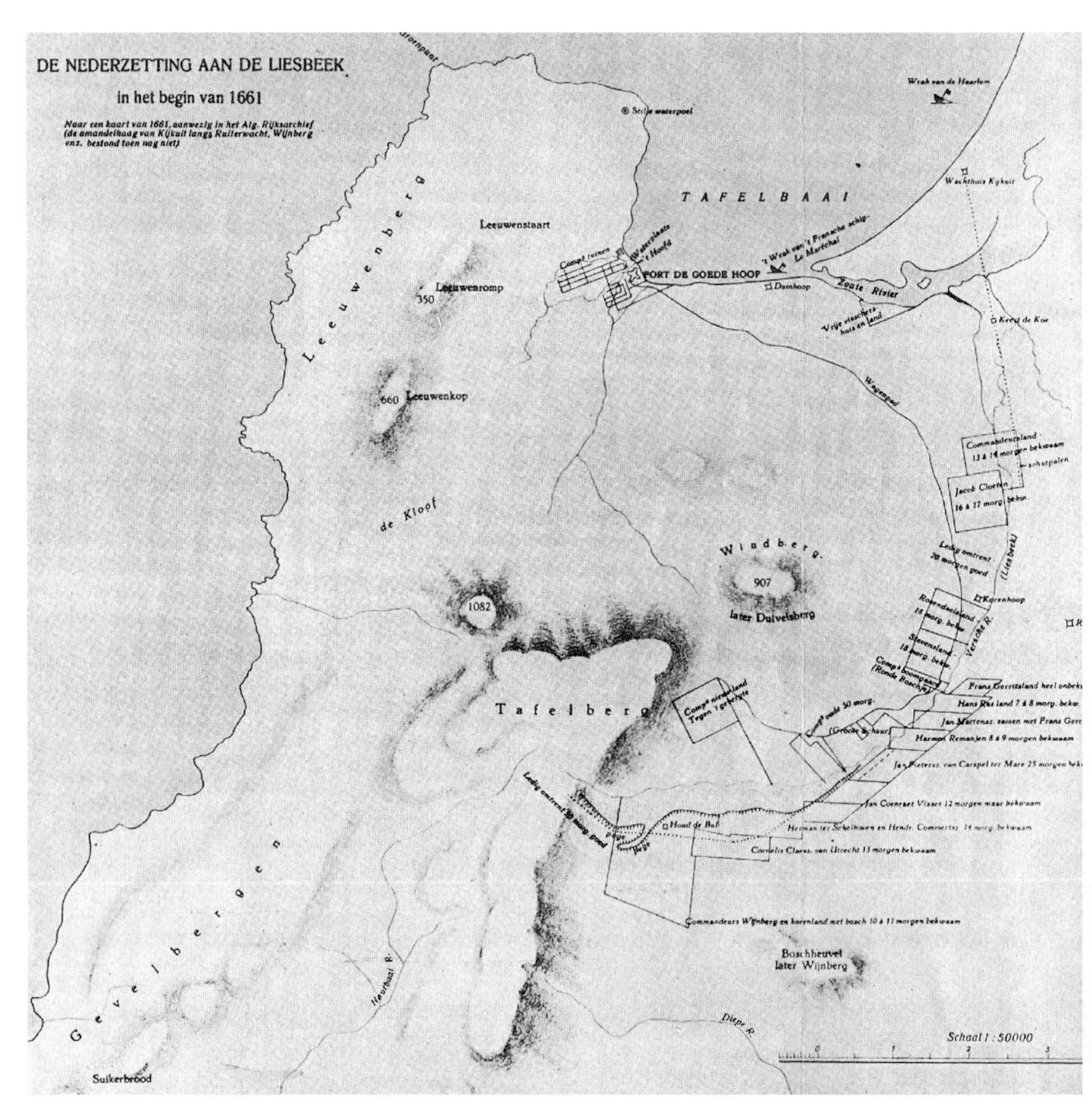

The settlement on the Liesbeeck River at the beginning of 1661, the year before Catharina married Hans Ras. His farm is shown on the lower bank of the Liesbeeck River in Rondebosch.

thanks to her nursing, Hans survived. The incident was reported to the officials the following day.

Such an incident was not at all unusual. In 17th-century Europe, swearing and physical fighting amongst both working-class men and women were common occurrences. In a fight, women often bit and pulled each other's hair. Men fought with knives to settle an argument, slitting their opponent's mouth halfway up their cheeks.

Catharina proved to be a hardworking and industrious farmer's wife and by all accounts appears to have made a difference to Hans's financial circumstances. By 1663, she and her husband had harvested nine and a half morgen of grain[48], and they owned livestock. Besides the property on the Liesbeeck River, the Ras family also owned a house on the town side of what is now Strand Street, which became a place for Hans and Catharina to stop over on business trips. The road which led from the farms in the Rondebosch area to Table Bay was often in a shocking condition. Hans and his neighbours were put in charge of the upkeep of the muddied, rutted road vital to the refreshment station and the farms.

Within a few years, Catharina had achieved every pioneer woman's goal: to become a successful landowning man's wife. But her habits were still those of a hardworking peasant. She gained a reputation of being wild and wilful. Besides riding around the farm alone, Catharina made trips to and from Table Bay on horseback to conduct business in the settlement, without a slave to accompany her. At the time, this was considered scandalous and dangerous behaviour for a woman.

48 A morgen was an old Dutch land measure equivalent to 0.857 hectares or two acres.

Indeed, the area was not safe: in 1666 there were so many lions prowling around the settlement and the nearby farmlands that the Company offered a reward of 25 guilders for each lion shot by a free burgher. Residents of the Cape hamlet complained that the roaring of lions on the slopes of Lions Head kept them awake at night. In 1671 there was a particularly bad drought: predators were starving while buck and other animals died from lack of grazing. Lions ventured onto the farmlands in broad daylight to snatch sheep and cattle. Hyaenas were chased out of the graveyard at the back of the fort where they dug up the corpses and ate them.

Hans was mauled by a lion while he was working on his farm, and the legend has it that Catharina jumped onto her horse in hot pursuit of the animal and shot it. Catharina nursed her husband after the attack, but without modern medicines such as anti-tetanus injections, there was little she could do. Hans died, and Catharina was left a widow with four children to support, the youngest not yet one year old. The best path was to marry again.

Almost a year later, in April 1672, she married Francois Champlaer. In contrast to Hans, he was an incompetent farmer and a bad businessman. He had been employed as a servant at an inn in Table Bay. Catharina's standard of living dropped. The once large farm now consisted of only 11 morgen and 400 square yards on which only 300 sheep and some other livestock grazed. For Catharina this marriage brought not only financial hardship but more heartbreak. The threat of Khoekhoe attacks was still ever-present, yet many white pioneers had not learnt their lesson. In January 1673, Francois and seven other burghers unlawfully went fishing and

A fanciful sketch of Lion's Head, drawn by Johan Jacobsz Saar when he spent four days at the Cape in 1660. Above the "lion" on the lower slopes. Lions roamed freely on the mount

e "table", and an elephant, a boar and other animals can be seen
the time.

hunting game at Macassar, Strandfontein, the territory owned by the Khoekhoe chief Gonnema. When they had still not returned by 29 July 1673, the Company declared them dead, presumably killed by Chief Gonnema's men.

Catharina's fourth husband was Laurens Cornelisz from Gothenburg. Socially and financially this was yet another step down the ladder for Catharina. Laurens was employed as a servant by Thielman Hendrickz, the man who had stabbed Hans Ras on his wedding day. Newly arrived from Germany, Laurens married Catharina three months after his arrival at the Cape. He was not a free burgher and owned no property; to him she must have been a prize. She still possessed two properties: the remainder of the original Ras farm on the Liesbeeck River and a house near the fort.

Catharina's next few years illustrate what it was like to be at the low end of the settler social and economic scale. The family was forced to sell most of the farm and move to the small house near the castle. In December 1676 the Company ordered the demolition of the houses built too near the castle walls – they were declared slum dwellings. In their place, a road to the southern peninsula would be constructed and additions added to the castle. The owners of the demolished houses were forcibly moved to small houses on the edge of the Company gardens, near present-day Kloof Street. Catharina and her family were some of the first victims of forced removal.

Instead of monetary compensation, Catharina and the other evicted homeowners were granted the right to sell "sugar and Cape brewed beers"[49] to make up for any loss of income from their property. But the family

49 Cairns, "Tryn Ras", p 26.

was still on the breadline: her husband was unemployed, and their new home was too small to start a market garden. Catharina gave birth to two daughters fathered by Laurens, Maria and Laurentia, but their father did not live to see them grow up. He was crushed to death by a charging elephant while out on a hippo-hunting trip. Catharina became a widow for the fourth time when baby Laurentia was only a few months old. This was not the end of tragedy for Catharina, as her daughter Maria Cornelisz died in early childhood. Left with children to feed, for the first time Catharina asked for help, and was given the Company grant to impoverished widows – a monthly rice ration.

The turn of the wheel

For Catharina Ras, Simon van der Stel helped to turn the wheel of fortune: she was one of the first residents to benefit from his policy of expansion. At the time of his arrival she had been widowed four times, had several small children, was living in a tiny house and was living off the Company rice ration. Van der Stel granted her a large piece of land at the foot of the Steenberg Mountains in the lush Constantia valley: 25 morgen on which to build a house and also to farm. (There is some suggestion that Catharina may have taken matters into her own hands and squatted on the vacant land, which made it easier for her to apply for it.) The land was probably granted to her as a form of a charity handout, like the land granted to the widows in the Tijgerberg area. Initially she had no legal title deed, probably because women were then not legally empowered to buy land. At the time, Van der Stel planned to build a house and also to farm on the large plot adjacent to hers; he would be her only neighbour. Part of the deal was that she would look after his cattle and allow them to graze on part of her land until his house Constantia was built. Catharina named her house Swaaneweide.

Catharina may have been wild but she was canny and practical. When Van der Stel decided to take residence on the newly completed Constantia property next door, she promptly requested that he give her an official title deed, just in case she fell out of favour and he wished to amalgamate the flourishing Swaaneweide property with his own. He granted her request and in 1688 the "Widow Ras" was officially awarded the plot of land.

Catharina married again for the fifth (and last) time on 25 January 1680. This husband, the German Matthys Michelsz, proved as industrious as Hans Ras. By 1692, after 15 years on Swaaneweide, Catharina and Matthys owned seven male slaves and one female slave. They had planted 8 000 vines as well as wheat, barley and rye. The farm also boasted 600 sheep and sundry other livestock numbering 140 animals.

In an age where etiquette and social restrictions governed women's lives, Catharina flouted every rule in the book. Mother of a brood of children, she let them run wild. In 1685, the VOC commissioner Baron van Reede described her children as resembling "Brazilian cannibals". He was shocked at their illiteracy and despaired that Catharina and her children were typical of the families he had met at the Cape, who ran wild in the countryside and never opened a book apart from the Bible. He was also horrified by their mother's custom of riding horses all over the countryside "bareback like an Indian". Not only did she ride without a saddle, she rode astride like a man. Baron van Reede maintained "she terrified anyone who met her en route" with her wild reckless fashion of riding, any man in her path gave her right of way immediately, and nobody would suspect that she was the wife of a well-off landowner because of her audacious behaviour. The only thing in Catharina's favour, in his eyes, was her warm and generous hospitality and flourishing farm, Swaaneweide. The Van Reede party were treated to a sumptuous lunch which included "radishes, freshly baked bread and beautiful cabbages".[50] Catharina informed Van Reede that she had thrice been plunged into dire poverty before enjoying her present circumstances, and hinted that she personally had avenged the deaths of her husbands.

Catharina's unorthodox behaviour does not seem to have perturbed Simon van der Stel; indeed it probably differed little from that of the other lower working-class women at the Cape with little time for social refinement. Nor would her unruly, illiterate children have troubled him. Not only were most of the children at the Cape illiterate, many parents were as well – her husband Michelsz signed documents with a cross. To Van der Stel, Catharina's worth was that she had turned a piece of uncultivated land into a flourishing farm, which he could exhibit to the commissioner, Baron van Reede, as a successful example of his policy of encouraging more free burghers to farm. Van der Stel had a farming population on his hands who were struggling, many living in dire poverty. According to the 1682 census, most households could barely support themselves. Out of the settler population of 92 men, 64 women and 162 children, half of the colony's wheat, barley and rye was produced by only 12 households. Self-supporting Catharina was one of Van der Stel's successes.

In 1695, at the age of about 55, Catharina sold the farm for 800 guilders to the wealthy Frederick Russouw, a member of the Burgher Council. With farming in her blood, however, she and Michelsz bought another farm named Weltevreden on the Berg River at Joostenberg, near the newly settled farmlands of Drakenstein. (In 1679, the first grazing rights in the interior had been granted to farmers by the Company.)

Van der Stel had good reasons for approving the purchase of the farm at Joostenberg. Unlike other free burghers, Catharina had proved her ability by turning the land at Swaanewiede into a flourishing farm. Van der Stel needed capable farmers like her to start cultivating fresh land to improve ailing food production at the Cape. Once again Catharina was a model settler, fitting in with Van der Stel's plans to expand into the interior and cultivate land further away from the original Cape settlement.

Catharina died in 1708 at the age of 66, and it is thought that she is buried on the farm at Joostenberg. By way of household possessions she did not leave much behind. Catharina and most of her Dutch, German and French Huguenot counterparts lived in sparsely furnished households, and her death inventory consisted of bedding and a few essential pieces of old furniture – two kists (wooden chests) and three old katels (beds with flaps to hold bedding). Catharina's main assets were an enormous number of useful farming tools and equipment, 12 slaves, income from wine and grain, 120 sheep and various other livestock: an

50 Van Reede tot Drakenstein, *Journaal van Zijn Verblife aan die Kaap*, pp 150-151.

The first church in the Drakenstein valley, from a sketch by Van Stade in 1710.

appropriate legacy for a hardworking farmer's wife, part of the large core of women who sustained the Cape agriculture-based economy.

Catharina's farm Swaanewiede is today the luxury hotel and golf course named Steenberg, and a restaurant on the property is named after this pioneering woman.

CHAPTER 8

The French Huguenots

The title deed of a Huguenot farm.

A tourist cannot visit the famous wine routes of the Cape, with their distinctive Cape Dutch farmhouses and world-class wines, without coming into contact with the names and stories of the French Huguenot women. The farms La Provence, La Motte, and La Rochelle are but a few in the collection of priceless heritage sites left to South Africa by the Huguenots; in each case, women were instrumental in their founding.

Simon van der Stel had some success in encouraging the expansion of free-burgher farms, and by 1687, wheat and fruit were cultivated as far as Stellenbosch and Drakenstein; but the Cape still needed more settlers to increase food production. In 1687 Van der Stel requested the VOC to send him Chinese workers from Batavia to set the "lazy" Dutch and German Cape farmers an example; but instead the VOC arranged for French Huguenot refugees to settle at the Cape.

The Huguenots were refugees who had fled religious persecution in France, often with only the clothes on their backs. Many of them were forced to relocate from country to country. They came from all regions of France, from all walks of life: peasants, farmers, tradesmen, artisans, surgeons, apothecaries and lawyers. One of the many restrictions placed on Protestants in France prohibited women from working as seamstresses or midwives. More inhumane was the law that six-year-old children were parted from their mothers and forced to live with Catholic neighbours. If the Protestant parents could not afford to pay for their board, the children were put in a poorhouse. Marriages between Protestants and Catholics were forbidden, and any offspring of such a marriage were considered to be illegitimate and forced to become Catholics.

The Huguenots had a reputation for making good quality wine, brandy and vinegar. Viticulture at the Cape was in its infancy and struggling, and the VOC saw profit in encouraging the Huguenots, whom they described as "industrious people, satisfied with little",[51] to relocate to the Cape. The plight of the Huguenots who reached Holland was desperate: most of them were penniless, having fled France with the bare essentials. An assisted immigration scheme was put in place to make settling at the Cape more attractive. The VOC offered free passage, advanced financial loans, allocated freehold land to any settler who wished to farm, loaned out farming implements, seed and livestock, and promised to send out a French minister to conduct church services. Nonetheless, only 200 French Huguenot families made the journey. The main body of refugees arrived over several months from April 1688 to May 1689 and more trickled in until about 1717.

In contrast to the first party of Dutch settlers in 1652, the Huguenots arrived at an established settlement. The small town boasted a stone castle with several houses clustered around it. Farms spread out in all directions from the town. Further inland another small village, Stellenbosch, had sprung up. However, Van der Stel had clamped down on the expansion of farming in the Stellenbosch area, which he considered fully settled by 1685. Instead, he offered land in the surrounding area of Drakenstein. Thereafter he granted new land and loan farms as far as what are now Wellington and Paarl. The Dutch settlers had named the Berg River valley beyond Paarl "Limit Valley": to them it was the end of civilization. When the Huguenots began to settle there, they named it Val du Charon or Wagonmakers Valley (Wagenmakersvallei), because the bulk of them were wainwrights.

Van der Stel supplied the French settlers with basic foodstuffs to tide them over until they could grow their own, as well as materials to build simple reed, mud and clay houses. The ground, though rich and fertile, had to be cleared and at first the Huguenots could not afford slave labour. Neither did they possess enough agricultural implements. Van der Stel applied to the VOC for funds to buy these essentials, and personally donated a span of oxen for ploughing. To transport goods to and from the Cape Port involved a long, dangerous and slow journey by ox wagon over rough sandy paths.

Initially, Van der Stel's project did not look as if it would succeed. Many of the refugees were skilled artisans and craftsmen and not farmers. As early as October 1688, a scant few months after the arrival of the first party of Huguenots, Van der Stel stated that the French fell far short of their reputation as hard workers and that he had to summon up all his Christian goodwill to deal with their constant demands. Furthermore, he had to supply them with more domestic stock to get their farms up and running than he had expected. Little had changed by 1699, when Van der Stel wrote to the VOC in the Netherlands that he did not wish to be burdened with more refugees because they "had a limited knowledge of farming, and exert themselves little about it, thus causing much poverty amongst themselves".[52]

51 Bryer & Theron, *The Huguenot Heritage*, p. 30.

52 Botha, *The French Refugees at the Cape*, p 160.

A view of the Paarl Mountain, from a sketch by Van Stade in 1710.

However, ten years later, many of the Huguenot farms boasted prosperous vineyards and orchards, and wheat, maize and cattle were all thriving. Their farms stretched from Stellenbosch through Olifantshoek, Paarl and on to Wagenmakersvallei. The name Olifantshoek changed to Le Coin Francais, and for a while the Huguenots called it La Petite Rochelle, but the Dutch name of Fransche Hoek stuck, eventually becoming modern-day Franschhoek.

Huguenot women contributed greatly to this success. Even if they did not own property, they worked alongside their husbands to make their farms thrive, and many widows managed productive farms. They often produced large families, swelling the population. The average number of children in the first Huguenot refugee families at the Cape was three and a half: by 1719 this had increased to over six.

Tensions at the Cape

Van der Stel's expectations of increased production had been fulfilled, but there was ongoing tension between him and the Huguenots. They wanted to preserve their language and customs, whereas Van der Stel wanted to integrate them with the Dutch community. Trouble reared its head in 1689 when the Huguenots asked Van der Stel's permission to govern their own church affairs and services. They wanted French spoken at every service, instead of alternating with Dutch. Van der Stel refused this request – at the time the Netherlands was at war with France and anti-French feeling was running high. (Furthermore, during the many campaigns of Louis XVII, Van der Stel had fought in the Dutch army against the French.) However, the Huguenots took their appeal further and the VOC approved their request. This resulted in services being held in a barn in Drakenstein, and the start of construction of a church in Paarl. (This was only finished in 1720. The Strooidak Church in Main Road, Paarl, replaced the old church building in 1805, and is now a national monument.)

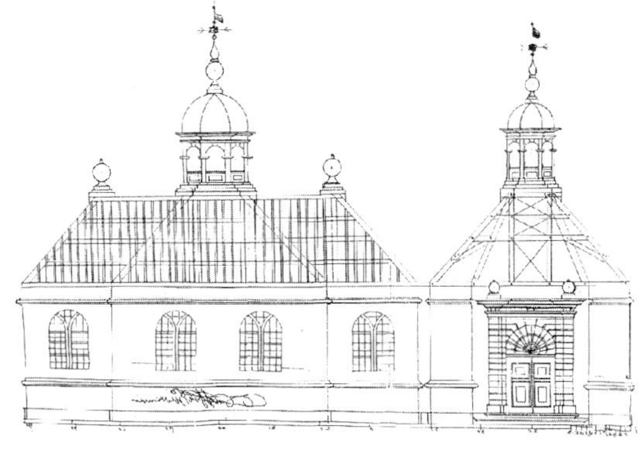
A diagram of the second church building used by the Drakenstein congregation. It stood on the site of the present Strooidak Church in Paarl.

Language remained a bone of contention with Van der Stel. The Reverend Simond applied to the VOC for French teachers and separate French schools. His request was granted in 1691, but the teachers that arrived were instructed to establish dual-medium schools for both Dutch and French pupils. Both languages were to be taught, emphasising Dutch, with the intention that the Huguenots would eventually blend into the Dutch community. The first Huguenots grimly tried to hold onto their culture, but when the Reverend Simond left the Cape in 1702, the Dutch authorities seized the chance to ban all church services in French, as well as the teaching of French in schools.

Initially, most Huguenots married into their own cultural group. Over the next few generations, however, the Huguenots became fully integrated into Dutch culture at the Cape, losing the use of French and joining the Dutch Reformed Church. Although the community at the Cape settlement in the early 18th century had started to spread out, it was still a close-knit one. One of the complaints of the Huguenots was that Van der Stel would not allow Huguenot properties to border each other. He allotted land to German and Dutch settlers between Huguenot farms, so there was little option but to mingle with the neighbours. Consequently intermarriage flourished between neighbours, friends and relatives.

Marie le Fevre: a long road to prosperity

Huguenot women were used to travelling, putting down roots and then having to move on once more with their families. For these hardy people, the Cape was just one more challenge to face. Even so, to make the journey to the Cape was a major undertaking, only for the desperate and the brave. Although many Huguenot women ended their lives in comfortable circumstances, they endured grinding poverty and hard work to achieve that goal.

A case in point is that of Marie le Fevre, who ended her life as a prosperous farmer's wife, but was widowed three times and lived in poverty for most of her life at the Cape. Marie married master wheelwright Charles Prevost; both lived in Calais. By the time the family set sail from Amsterdam in 1688 on *De Schelde*, Marie had three children and was heavily pregnant. The discomfort of the voyage for a pregnant woman can only be imagined – still less the experience of giving birth on board, as Marie did, to her youngest son Jacob.

De Schelde ran into heavy seas and put into a harbour in the Cape Verde Islands to repair the damage, but left almost immediately because of the danger of pirates operating in the area. She suffered further damage after running into a heavy storm, but managed to reach the Cape after a 15-week voyage. After safely making the harrowing journey, the family disembarked on 29 May 1688.

In July 1688 Charles died, and Marie was left a penniless widow in a strange land, with four small children to feed. With almost indecent haste, she married again on 29 August 1688, taking a German, Henrich Eckhoff, as her second husband – obviously a practical move. The couple moved to Drakenstein, so at least Marie was amongst her fellow refugees. As a "poor French fugitive",[53] to help her establish her family she was awarded the sum of 450 rix dollars.

When her second husband died in 1692, Marie was better off than during her first

53 De Villiers, "Marie le Fevre", p 181.

widowhood, but still not able to comfortably support her children. She owned oxen, sheep, cows and land with a harvest of eight bags of wheat and one of rye, which together with farm implements and household effects amounted to 2 200 guilders. However, her debts amounted to 1 300 guilders, not unusual for a free burgher. To establish themselves, burghers were forced to borrow money for implements and other farm necessities from the Company and many found it difficult to repay their debts, their farms needing constant capital investment.

There was only one solution. Two months later, on 19 October 1692, Marie married yet again: an ex-soldier, Louis de Peronne, who hailed from Flanders. He proved to be a good farmer. A vineyard was laid out and the livestock increased. But once again Marie was destined to face hardship. De Peronne died in 1696 after four years of marriage. This time she married a fellow Huguenot, Hercules de Pres, an old friend who had made the journey out with her on the *De Schelde* in 1688. Hercules's sister, Elizabeth, had stood as a sponsor on board *De Schelde* at the baptism of Marie's son Jacob. An established and excellent farmer, Hercules extended the farm and it prospered.

In the case of Marie's family, Van der Stel's plan of integrating the Huguenots with their Dutch and German neighbours had born fruit. Marie's genes run through the families of Provost, Van der Merwe, Eckhoff, Mostert, Brits, Du Preez and Van Schalkwyk.

Maria Mouton: love and murder

Despite the rigid adherence by most Huguenots to a strict moral code, there were of course exceptions. Van der Stel, in his litany of complaints about the Huguenots, grumbled that "some of them are ill behaved".[54] His criticism was well grounded; in the early 1700s the Rev Simond became extremely concerned about the lapse in morals amongst the new settlers and urged the Church Council to enforce strict punishment on those who strayed.

On the whole, liaisons between whites were mostly condoned by the community but the case was entirely different when a female member of the community strayed and had a blatant affair with a man of colour, and her own slave at that. Maria Mouton went one step further. On 3 January 1714, she and her slave lover, Titus of Bengal, murdered her husband. Her defence was that during her nine years of marriage to Franz Jooste, he constantly ill-treated her and had never allowed her to acquire any new clothes. The family was probably poverty-stricken. Both Maria's sisters married poor struggling farmers who all farmed in the same vicinity of the Jooste farm, Vier-en-twintigriviere, and her father, Jacques, struggled to make a living.

Franz Jooste also possessed a violent temper; Maria, Titus and their co-accused, Fortyn of Bengal, all testified that on the day he died, he had argued with Maria and threatened to strike her. She fled for protection to Titus, who took a rifle from the house and shot Jooste. Fortyn, who witnessed this event, realised that Jooste was only wounded and took a piece of a wood and iron ploughshare and beat him to death. The willingness of the two men to defend their mistress suggests that Jooste was a man who abused his slaves; they were only too ready to seek revenge. When the conspirators heard a horseman approaching, they tied Jooste's body to a horse and dragged it to a porcupine burrow, where they buried it. Maria told the horse-

54 Botha, *The French Refugees at the Cape*, p 160.

Typical dress of Huguenot women in the 17th century. The woman on the left is working-class, while the other two women are wealthier. The workaday clothes of the working-class French Huguenot women was similar to the clothing of their Dutch and German counterparts. However, the more formal or wealthier women's clothes were simpler than those of the Dutch. Although the bodices were tight fitting, the dresses were less rigid with bustles instead of hoops and soft frills instead of starched collars and cuffs.

man, Visagie, that her husband had gone to search for lost cattle. Much later she reported to the Landdrost that her husband had not returned from his search for the missing cattle.

A search was launched, but by the time they discovered Jooste's grave, only his bones were left; all other body parts had been devoured by wild animals. However, neighbours testified that it was common knowledge that Maria had been carrying on a "disgraceful" affair with Titus for many months before the murder.

Dutch justice was harsh. They were all sentenced to death. Maria was half strangled, tortured with branding irons and then strangled until she died. Titus was impaled on a stake and left to die slowly. Fortyn had his right hand chopped off and was then impaled. The heads and hands of both the slaves' corpses were stuck on poles at the border of the Jooste farm as warning to slaves who planned a similar deed. The Huguenot community also took their revenge on the "disgrace" that Maria had brought upon them: her father was never allowed to stand for election to the Church Council or the local Heemraad (a court dealing with minor disputes). The Joostes' two young sons were placed in the care of their grandfather and their step-grandmother. One of Maria's descendants was the famous writer Laurens van der Post.

Elizabeth Joubert: scandalous rumours

The case of Elizabeth Joubert was treated very differently when brought before the Council, probably because her affair was with a fellow Huguenot, and both of them were free burghers from affluent backgrounds.

When she set sail from Rotterdam aboard the *Berg China* on 20 March 1688, Elizabeth was 20 years old and married to Pierre Malan, but when she landed at the Cape on 4 August 1688, she was married to Pierre Joubert of Provence. Both Malan and Joubert's wife Susanne Reyne died during the voyage to the Cape. The practical Pierre promptly married his fellow passenger on board the ship, soon after their spouses' bodies had been committed to the deep.

The Cape proved to be financially profitable for Elizabeth and Pierre. Their farms thrived: La Provence grew good vines. In 1708 they acquired the farm La Plaisante Plaats in the Worcester district, and a third farm, La Motte in the Franschhoek Valley, was bought in 1709. A fifth and last farm, L'Ormarins, which they acquired in 1719, already had vast flourishing vineyards. Fate had dealt Elizabeth a winning hand as far as material possessions were concerned when she married Pierre at sea.

In the love stakes, however, it appears she was not as lucky. The family was preparing to celebrate the wedding of Elizabeth's daughter, her namesake Elizabeth, to Guilliaume Loret on January 23 1707, when the officiating minister, Reverend Beck, informed them that he refused to use the normal wedding vows at the ceremony. It had come to his ears that the mother of the bride had been having a long-standing passionate affair with her daughter's future husband. At this, her husband took great umbrage, believing his wife's protestations that the rumour was false. He attempted to have the Reverend Beck removed and approached the Church Council on the matter. He failed, and the Council stated that the story was not just a rumour but common knowledge in the community. The young couple were married with modified vows.

Catherine Marais: death for a few unripe melons

On 13 April 1688, Catherine Taboureux, her husband Charles Marais and their four children arrived at Saldanha Bay on the *Voorschooten*. The passengers were taken to Table Bay on the cutter *Jupiter*. The Marais family were one of many who had been forced to convert to Catholicism in France. They fled first to The Hague in the Netherlands, where they rejected Catholicism and joined the Protestant Walloon Church. Another reason for their flight from France was that Catherine and Charles came from the Hurepoix region of the Ille de France, where the Catholic bourgeoisie had appropriated large tracts of farmland, leaving farmers, peasants and tradesmen destitute. Catherine and Charles settled on land in Drakenstein and named their farm after their home in France, Le Plessis Marle.

The Huguenots arrived at a time when the Cape settlement was expanding, which meant more land was being settled and cultivated by European farmers and there was less land for the Khoekhoen to hunt and graze their livestock. Khoekhoe men were employed by the Huguenot farmers on a migrant-worker basis. Many Khoekhoe women worked as servants, and often learnt to speak French. However, the relationship was not always easy, and sometimes erupted into violence. At the end of their first year's residence, Charles was stoned to death on his farm by Edissa, also known as Dikkop, a Khoekhoe man, because Charles refused to let him pick his unripe melons. Why would Edissa murder Marais merely to gain a few green watermelons? Hunger, frustration at the loss of traditional grazing lands, and the Khoekhoe tradition of sharing with those less fortunate could certainly have been factors.

Fortunately, Catherine Marais had two grown sons to help out, and she ran the farm so successfully that the property stayed in the family for generations.

Cornelia Villon: taking a stand

Although women had no say in official matters, they were not meek bystanders allowing officialdom to run the course of their lives. Many Huguenot women played an active part in resisting Catholic oppression in France: in 1664 in the Dauphine area in the South of France and in 1665 in Poitou, women played a key role in preventing Catholic soldiers from demolishing Protestant churches.

Huguenot women certainly took a stand in protesting against the administration of Willem Adriaan van der Stel. In 1699, Simon van der Stel retired from his post as Governor of the Cape, partly on the grounds of ill health. On the whole he was a very capable governor and the Cape flourished under his administration. However his son, Willem Adriaan van der Stel, who was appointed as the next Governor, was different. He built himself a magnificent farmhouse, Vergelegen (in modern day Somerset West), and spent several weeks at a time at this country estate, neglecting his work at the castle. He used Company slaves on his farm, and instituted a monopoly on the sale of wine, grain, meat and farm produce, enriching himself and a small circle of Company officials. There were several plots to rid the Cape of Van der Stel, and he retaliated by imprisoning the ringleaders in the castle and on ships anchored out in Table Bay. Willem van der Stel also made a more concerted effort than his father to eradicate French language and customs.

Cornelia Villon fought back against this

A view of Vergelegen, the beautiful farm built by Willem Adriaan van der Stel on 400 morgen of land granted him by the Company's Commissioner. (A plan of the property appears on the opposite page.) Van der Stel's farm produce competed with the free burghers', causing them to complain to the Directorate in Holland about his lavish lifestyle. Van der Stel was suspended from office and returned to the Netherlands.

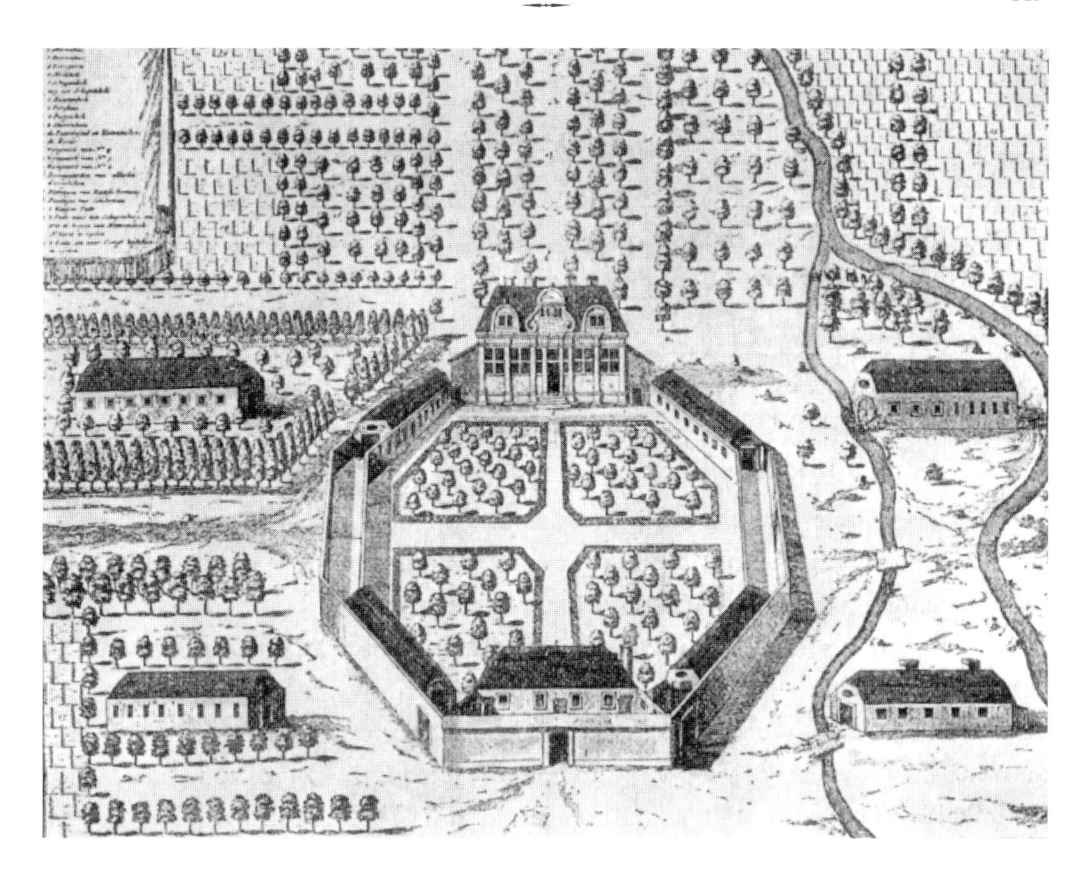

corrupt government. Her husband, Hercules des Pres, was a prominent social figure and one of the leaders of the resistance campaign to overthrow Van der Stel. She twice helped him to escape from Van der Stel's soldiers. After he and a fellow conspirator were arrested on 28 May 1709, the Governor received a petition from the "bedrukte vroue"[55] of the prisoners, stating that they were not allowed any access to their husbands. Women were running large farms and argued that they needed the advice of their husbands. Van der Stel ignored the petition. Cornelia continued running the farm until Hercules was finally released and Van der Stel was sent back to the Netherlands in disgrace.

55 Fouche, *The Diary of Adam Tas*, p xxix.

The push into the interior

The Huguenots were in the forefront of the push into the interior and the start of the trekboer movement. By the start of the 18th century, Dutch, German and French settlers had cultivated the land as far as the Hottentots Holland Mountains. The number of stock farmers had increased, which meant they needed to seek new pasturage, and Willem Adriaan van der Stel decreed that the land beyond the Hottentots Holland and to the north of the Cape settlement be cultivated or used for stock farming. The Cape settlement began to spread out as farmers packed up their entire households and moved farther into the interior. Dutch, German and Huguenot families all became trekboers, and this led to a further integration of cultures. Usually it was the poorer farmers who migrated in order to find a better life, while the more prosperous remained at the Cape.

There was a natural progression from the first Huguenot pioneers who "pushed the limits" of the Cape settlement as far as Wagenmaakersvallei, to their descendants who became trekboers. For example, Marie Mouy, born in 1685, arrived at the Cape in 1699 from Orleans with her father Pierre and sister Jeanne on the *Donkervliet*. Pierre established the farm Welvanpas in Wagenmakersvallei. In 1700 the 15-year-old Marie married 37-year old Francois Retief, a Huguenot who had also come from Orleans with his sister Anne. He owned the farm Patats Kloof at the foot of the Habiquasberg in Wagenmakersvallei. Marie lived to be what was a ripe old age in those days, dying on 21 September 1758. She bore nine children, and her daughter Madelaine lived to the age of 97. Marie became the matriarch of the Retief family, and her grandson was the Voortrekker leader Piet Retief.

A miniature painting of a lady, c. 1650, with 14 mica transparencies that can be laid over it to change its dress, mood and even sex. This charming toy belonged to the Retief family.

Conclusion

The 17th century at the Cape was a turbulent one, offering many challenges and opportunities for women. By the close of the century, the Cape had grown into a substantial settlement, with three-storey houses, cobbled streets, shops, neatly cultivated farms and flourishing economies.

The Cape at the end of the 17th century was a melting-pot of nationalities, colours and creeds. Fresh infusions of French Huguenot refugees and a small, steady stream of Dutch, German, Scandinavian and Flemish settlers had swelled the European population at the Cape. As the need for labour increased, more slave women were brought into the country. There was still a chronic shortage of marriageable white women, and in 1688, Baron van Reede encouraged European men to marry slave women of mixed origin. A growing trickle of Khoekhoe women worked as servants in the homes of the European settlers.

The population was still small, and interaction between all these groups of women occurred daily. The majority of women, regardless of colour or nationality, were engaged in housework and rearing children; many worked in the fields, in diary farming or in other kinds of agriculture. But this did not have a levelling effect on society as a whole. Society was still stratified into the rich and the poor, with the Europeans and a few free blacks at the top, and at the bottom of the pile the slaves and the Khoekhoe servants. At the end of the 17th century there was a degree of racial mixing in Cape society, but strictly on the basis of marriages of manumitted slave women, usually of mixed parentage, to white men. Most free blacks and manumitted slave women lived on the breadline, and were not socially acceptable in "white" society. Even the ownership of land did not automatically grant them entry to these circles.

Khoekhoe women integrated even less with the white population. The concept of land ownership was culturally foreign to them, and there was little desire to mix in European circles. Unlike the slave women, who desperately needed to improve their financial and social status, initially many Khoekhoe women were secure in their clan system. However, by the end of the 17th century, time was beginning to run out: the clan system and the age-old Khoekhoe way of life were rapidly vanishing. While white settlers moved into the interior and claimed more Khoekhoe traditional grazing lands, trade to the East increased with ships bringing deadly diseases such as smallpox. In the 18th century this fatal disease would decimate the Khoekhoe population, disintegrating the clans and causing the survivors to increasingly seek work in European homesteads and on farms. By and large, interaction between Khoekhoe women and the European community remained on a servant and mistress basis.

For the European settlers, gaining a foothold in society was easier than for any other group. In accordance with the VOC's plan for more free burghers to be involved in agriculture, a few established residents such as Catharina

Ras and Tryntjie and Beatrix Verwey had risen from poverty to own thriving farms. Land ownership was firmly in the hands of the European population (only a few free blacks held land). Nonetheless, many Huguenot, Dutch and German settlers were on the breadline.

Willem Adriaan van der Stel's administration and a growing population created a need for more cultivated land, and farmers moved further inland. They became part of the new settler movement, the trekboers, in the years to follow. This migration led to a further integration of French language and culture with Dutch and German, as trekboer families settled in isolated areas and intermarried.

Women of all backgrounds would be part of the push into the interior. Slaves, Khoekhoe servants, Europeans and manumitted wives and daughters all trekked into the unknown to cultivate new farmland, establish homes and adapt to a new ways – which included encountering black African communities. From the 18th century onwards, the first intensive interaction took place between the white trekboers, black groups and the Bushman people.

For Bushman women, the impact of European settlement had so far not been extreme; but this was soon to change. In the 18th century, when white colonists began to move further into the interior, the Bushmen were forced out of their traditional territory. The trekboer movement posed a serious threat to the survival of the Bushmen, who would ultimately be pushed to almost total destruction.

While the outlook for 17th-century women was at times bleak, many took advantage of the opportunities at the Cape and created better lives for themselves. When Simon van der Stel said that women were like jewels, he was of course meaning only European women; but the golden threads in the Cape tapestry were woven by all its women, from many different backgrounds. Without them, the Cape settlement could not have survived to meet the challenges of the 18th century.

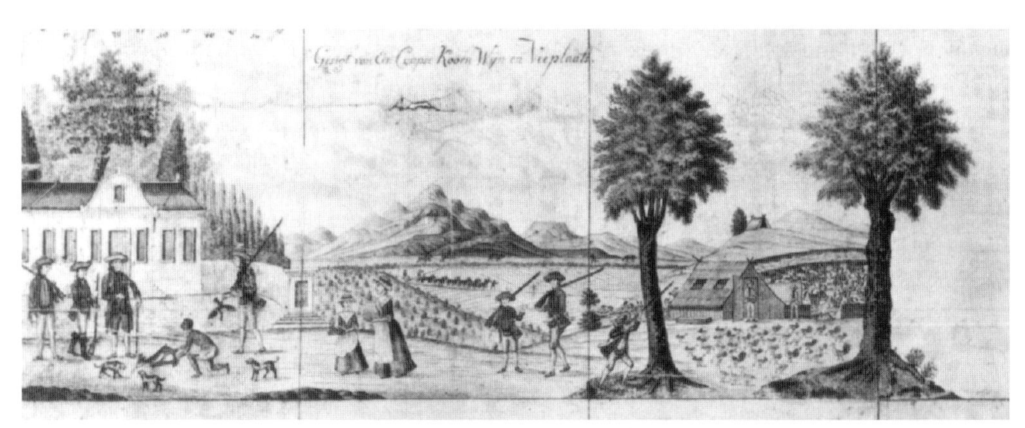

View of a Cape wheat, wine and cattle farm in 1780.

Bibliography

INTRODUCTION

Cape Archives, *Outgoing Letters,* 29th June 1691.

R C Shell, *Children of Bondage: a social history of the slave society of the Cape of Good Hope 1652-1838,* Newfoundland, Wesleyan Unversity Press, 1994.

H B Thom, ed., *Journal of Jan van Riebeeck,* Cape Town, A.A. Balkema for the Van Riebeeck Society, 1954.

CHAPTER 1. ***The Bushman gatherers***

J Barrow, *An Account of the Travels of Sir John Barrow in the Interior of South Africa*: 1797-1798, New York, G F Hopkins, 1802.

H J Deacon & J Deacon, *Human Beginnings in South Africa: uncovering the secrets of the Stone Age,* Cape Town, David Philip, 1999.

J Deacon, *Some Views on Rock Paintings in the Cederberg,* Cape Town, National Monuments Council, 1998.

J Deacon & T A Dowson, eds, *Voices from the Past: /Xam Bushmen and the Bleek and Lloyd collection,* Johannesburg, University of the Witwatersrand Press, 1996.

J Deacon, *Arrows as Agents of Belief amongst the /Xam Bushmen,* Cape Town, South African Museum, 1992.

E J Dunn, *The Bushmen,* London, Charles Griffin & Co, 1931.

R Elphick & H Giliomee, eds, *The Shaping of South African Society 1652-1820,* Cape Town, Maskew Miller Longman, 1984.

R Inskeep, *The Peopling of South Africa,* Cape Town, David Philip, 1978.

K Keuthmann, *Social organization of the !K¢ Bushmen,* Koln, Rudiger Koppe Verlag, 1994.

R B Lee, *The !Kung San: men, women and work in a foraging society,* New Rochelle, Cambridge University Press, 1982.

R B Lee, *The Dobe Ju/'hoans,* Toronto, Harcourt Brace College Publishers, 1993.

D N Lee & H C Woodhouse, *Art on the Rocks of Southern Africa,* Cape Town, Purnell & Sons, 1970.

A M Levin, ed., *The Cape Journals of Lady Anne Barnard 1797-1798,* Cape Town, Van Riebeeck Society, 1994 for 1993, 2nd series no 24.

J D Lewis-Williams, *Stories that Float from Afar,* Cape Town, David Philip, 2000.

J D Lewis-Williams & T A Dowson, *Rock Paintings of the Natal Drakensberg,* Pietermaritzberg, University of Natal, 1992.

J D Lewis-Williams & T A Dowson, *Images of Power,* Halfway House, Southern Book Publishers, 1999.

A C Myburgh, ed., *Anthropology for Southern Africa,* Pretoria, J L van Schaik, 1981.

J D Omer-Cooper, *History of Southern Africa,* Cape Town, David Philip, 1994.

P T Robertshaw, "The Origin of Pastoralism in the Cape", *South African Historical Journal,* 10, 1978.

P Skotnes, *Miscast: negotiating the presence of the Bushmen,* Cape Town, University of Cape Town Press, 1996.

A Smith, "Origins of the Bushmen of South Africa", *Gentleman's Magazine,* July, 1831.

A Smith, *The Journal of Andrew Smith and George Chapman,* Cape Town, Van Riebeeck Society, 1837.

H P Steyn, *Vanished Lifestyles: the early Cape Khoikhoi and San,* Pretoria, Unibook Publishers, 1990.

G M Theal, *History of South Africa before 1505,* Cape Town, C Struik, 1964.

H B Thom, op. cit.

M Wilson & L Thompson, eds, *The Oxford History of South Africa I : South Africa to 1870,* New York, Yale University Press, 1990.

B Woodhouse, *The Rock Art of the Golden Gate and Clarens District,* Rivonia, William Waterman Publications, 1996.

CHAPTER 2. ***The Khoekhoe cattle-herders***

Anonymous, *The Cape of Good Hope: a review of its present position to the intending settler, by a traveller,* Glasgow, David Byrne, 1744.

A Barnard, *Hunters & Herders of Southern Africa: a comparative ethnography of the Khoisan peoples,* Cambridge, Cambridge University Press, 1992.

J Barrow, op. cit.

E Boonzaaier, C Malherbe , A Smith & P Berens, eds, *The Cape Herders: a history of the Khoikhoi of Southern Africa,* Cape Town, David Philip, 1996.

H C Bredenkamp, A B I Flegg & H E F Pludderman, eds, *The Genadendal Dairies: diaries of the Herrenhut missionaries H Marsveld, D Schwinn, J C Kunel*, vol I (1792-1794), Bellville, University of the Western Cape Institute for Historical Research, 1992.

T Cameron & S B Spies, *An Illustrated History of South Africa*, Johannesburg, Jonathan Ball, 1987.

J Cope, *King of the Hottentots*, Cape Town, Howard Timmins, 1967.

T R H Davenport, *South Africa: a modern history*, Johannesburg, Macmillan, South Africa, 1987.

H J Deacon & J Deacon, *Human beginnings in South Africa: Uncovering the secrets of the Stone Age*, Cape Town, David Philip, 1999.

R Elphick, *Kraal and Castle: the Khoikoi and the founding of white South Africa*, New Haven, Yale University Press, 1977.

R Elphick & H Giliomee, op. cit.

J A Engelbrecht, *The Korana*, Cape Town, Maskew Miller, 1936.

M Hall, *The Changing Past: farmers, kings and traders in Southern Africa 200-1860*, Cape Town, David Philip, 1987.

A E Hooton, "Some early drawings of Hottentot women", Massachusetts, reproduced in booklet from the Peabody Musem of Salem.

R G Klein, "The Prehistory of Stone Age Herders in the Cape Province of South Africa", S A Archaeological Society Bulletin, 5, 1986.

P Kolben, *The Present State of the Cape of Good Hope*, vol I, London, Innys & Maney R, 1728.

R Raven-Hart, *Before van Riebeeck*, Cape Town, C Struik, 1967.

I Schapera, *The Khoisan Peoples of South Africa: Bushmen and Hottentots*, London, George Routledge & Sons, 1950.

E M Shaw, *The Hottentots*, Cape Town, The South African Museum, 1972.

A Smith & R Pheiffer, *The Khoikhoi at the Cape of Good Hope: seventeenth century drawings in the South African Library*, Cape Town, South African Library, 1993.

H P Steyn, *op. cit.*

G M Theal, *Ethnography and condition of South Africa before AD 1505*, London, George Allen & Unwin Ltd, 1922.

H B Thom, op. cit.

H J van Aswegen, *Geskiedenis van Suid-Afrika*, Pretroria, Academica, 1989.

CHAPTER 3. ***Krotoa***

A J Böeseken, *Jan van Riebeeck en sy Gesin*, Cape Town, Tafelberg, 1974.

Cape Archives: Resolution of the Council of Policy, 4 & 5 March 1670.

Cape Archives: Attestation of Hendrick Barentsz van Leewarden & Hans Conrad Veugelein, 21 August 1666.

R Elphick, op. cit.

R Elphick & H Giliomee, op. cit.

J A Heese & R T J Lombard, *South African Genealogies*, Pretoria, Human Sciences Research Council, 1986-2002.

C J F Muller, *500 Years: A History of South Africa*, Cape Town, Academica, 1984.

R Raven-Hart, op. cit.

Reader's Digest, *Illustrated History of South Africa*, Cape Town, Reader's Digest Association, 1994.

A Smith & R Pheiffer, *The Khoikhoi at the Cape of Good Hope: seventeenth century drawings in the South African Library*, Cape Town, South African Library, 1993.

G M Theal, 1964, op. cit.

H B Thom, op. cit.

H J van Aswegen, op. cit. 1989.

CHAPTER 4. ***Company wives***

Afrikaanse Kultuurvereeniginge, *Afrikaanse Kultuuralmanak*, Johannesburg, Afrikaanse Kultuurvereeniginge, 1980.

A J Böeseken, *Simon van der Stel en sy Kinders*, Cape Town, Nasou, 1964.

A J Böeseken, *1974*, op. cit.

A J Böeseken, *Slaves and Free Blacks at the Cape 1658-1700*, Cape Town, Tafelberg, 1977.

E C G Molsbergen, *Jan van Riebeeck en sy Tyd*, Pretoria, J L van Schaik, 1968.

H W J Picard, *Masters of the Castle*, Cape Town, C Struik, 1972.

K Schoeman, *Armosyn van die Kaap: voorspel tot vestiging, 1415-1651*, Cape Town, Human & Rousseau, 1999.

K Schoeman, *Armosyn van die Kaap: die wêreld van 'n slavin, 1652-1733*, Cape Town, Human & Rousseau, 2001.

H B Thom, op. cit.

Information from the official guide of the Groote Kerk, 2003.

CHAPTER 5. ***Enduring slavery***

A J Böeseken, 1977, op. cit.

A J Böeseken, 1974, op. cit.

D B Bosman, *Briewe van Johanna Maria van Riebeeck en ander Riebeeckiana*, Amsterdam, D Bosman, 1952.

G Botha, *A General History and Social Life at the Cape of Good Hope*, Cape Town, C Struik, 1962.

F Bradlow & M Cairns, *Early Cape Muslims*, Cape Town, A A Balkema, 1978.

Y da Costa & A Davids, *Pages from Muslim History*, Pietermaritzburg, Shuter & Shooter, 1994.

P Dane & S A Wallace, *The Great Houses of Constantia*, Cape Town, Don Nelson, 1981.

A Davids, *The Words that the Slaves Made*, Cape Town, Department of History, University of Cape Town, 1989.

H Deacon, ed., *The Island: a history of Robben Island 1488-1990*, Cape Town, University of the Western Cape, 1996.

C de Villiers & C Pama, *Genealogy of the Old Cape families*, Cape Town, A A Balkema, 1981.

R Elphick & H Giliomee, op. cit.

C L Engelbrecht, *Money in South Africa*, Cape Town, Tafelberg, 1987.

J L Hattingh, "Die Blanke Nageslag van Louis van Bengal en Lijsbeth van der Kaap", *Kronos*, 3, 1980.

H F Heese, *Groep sonder Grense: die rol en status van die gemengde bevolking van die Kaap 1652-1795*, Bellville, University of the Western Cape, 1984.

J A Heese & R T J Lombard, op. cit.

E M Mahida, *History of the Muslims in South Africa: a chronology*, Durban, Arabic Study Circle, 1992.

J S Marais, *The Cape Coloured People 1652-1937*, Johannesburg, Witwatersrand University Press, 1957.

K McKenzie, *The Making of an English Slave Owner: Samuel Eusebius Hudson at the Cape of Good Hope 1796-1807*, Cape Town, University of Cape Town Press, 1993.

C J F Muller, op. cit.

A C Partridge, *Lives, Letters & Diaries*, Cape Town, Purnell, 1971.

Reader's Digest, *An Illustrated History of South Africa*, Cape Town, The Reader's Digest Association, 1989.

R Ross, *Cape of Torment: slavery and resistance in South Africa*, London, Routledge & Kegan Paul, 1983.

K Schoeman, 1999, op. cit.

K Schoeman, 2001, op. cit.

R C Shell, "The Establishment and Spread of Islam from the Beginning of Company Rule to 1838", Essay as part of BA Honours Degree in History, University of Cape Town, 1974.

R C Shell, "From Rites to Rebellion: Islamic conversion, urbanization, and ethnic identities at the Cape of Good Hope, 1792 to 1904", *Canadian Journal of History*, 28(3), 1993.

R C Shell, 1994, op. cit.

R C Shell, "The Lodge Women of Cape Town, 1671 to 1795", Lecture given at the "Conference on Slavery and Forced Labour" at the University of Avignon, France, 16-18 October 2002.

G M Theal, *History of South Africa before 1793*, Cape Town, C Struik, 1922.

H B Thom, op. cit.

H Volgraaff, *The Dutch East India Company's Slave Lodge at the Cape*, Cape Town, South African Cultural Museum, 1999.

N Worden, *Slavery in Dutch South Africa*, Cambridge, Cambridge University Press, 1985.

N Worden & C Crais, eds, *Breaking the Chains*, Johannesburg, Witwatersrand University Press, 1994.

N Worden, R Versveld, D Dyer & C Bickford Smith, *The Chains that Bind Us: a history of slavery at the Cape*, Cape Town, Juta & Co, 1996.

CHAPTER 6. ***Working women***

Afrikaanse Kultuurvereeniginge, op. cit.

A J Böeseken, 1974, op. cit.

P Brooke Simons, *Cape Dutch Houses*, Cape Town, C Struik, 1987.

L Bryer & F Theron, *The Huguenot Heritage: the story of the Huguenots at the Cape*, Diep River, Chameleon Press, 1987.

J Burman, *1652 and so forth*, Cape Town, Human & Rousseau, 1973.

M Cairns, "Tryn Ras", *Familia*, XVI(2), 1979.

Cape Archives: Resolution of the Council of Policy, 4 & 5 March 1670.

Cape Archives: Attestation of Hendrick Barentsz van Leewarden & Hans Conrad Veugelein, 21 August 1666.

R Coetzee, *Spys en Drank: die oorsprong van die Afrikaanse eetkultuur*, Cape Town, C Struik, 1977.

P Dane & S A Wallace, op. cit.

N M du Plessis, ed., *The Tygerberg*, Cape Town, Tafelberg, 1998.

R Elphick & H Giliomee, op. cit.

L Guelke & R Shell, "An Early Landed Gentry: land and

wealth in the Cape Colony 1682-1731", *Journal of Historical Geography*, 9(3), 1983.

J A Heese, "Ons en ons Stamouers", *Familia*, XV(1), 1978.

J A Heese & R T J Lombard, op. cit.

H C V Leibrandt, *Precis of the Archives of the Cape of Good Hope*, Cape Town, W A Richards, 1901.

H W J Picard, op. cit.

C Pretorius, *Al Laggende en Pratende: Kaapse vroue in die 17de en 18de eeu*, Cape Town, Human & Rousseau, 1998.

K Schoeman, 1999, op. cit.

K Schoeman, 2001, op. cit.

R C Shell, 1994, op. cit.

R Shell & A Whyte, compilers, *The De La Fontaine Report: January 1732*, New Haven, S.N., 1990.

H B Thom, op. cit.

P J van der Merwe, *The Migrant Farmer in the History of the Cape Colony 1657-1842*, Athens, Ohio University Press, 1995.

N Worden, E Van Heyningen & V Bickford Smith, *Cape Town: the making of a city*, Cape Town, David Philip, 1998.

CHAPTER 7. ***Catharina Ras***

P Brooke Simons, op. cit.

M Cairns, "Tryn Ras" *Familia*, XV(1), 1978; XVI(1,2), 1979.

P Dane & S A Wallace, op. cit.

C L Engelbrecht, op. cit.

L Guelke & R Shell, op. cit.

K Schoeman, 1999, op. cit.

R C Shell, 1994, op. cit.

P J van der Merwe, op. cit.

H A van Reede tot Drakenstein, *Journaal van Zijn Verblife aan die Kaap*, Utrecht, Kemink & Zoon & V, 1941.

N Worden, E Van Heyningen & V Bickford Smith, *Cape Town: The making of a city*, Cape Town, David Philip Publishers, op. cit.

CHAPTER 8. ***The French Huguenots***

A J Böeseken, 1964, op. cit.

C G Botha, *The French Refugees at the Cape*, Cape Town, Cape Times Ltd, 1919.

M Boucher, *French Speakers at the Cape: The European Background*, Pretoria, UNISA, 1981.

P Brooke Simons, op. cit.

L Bryer & F Theron, op. cit.

M Cairns, "Cornelia Villon", *Familia*, XXIX(3,4), 1993.

P Coertzen, *Die Huguenote van Suid-Afrika 1688-1988*, Cape Town, Tafelberg, 1988.

W de Villiers, "Marie Le Fevre", *Familia*, XXVII(3), 1991.

C de Villiers & C Pama, op. cit.

R Elphick & H Giliomee, op. cit.

L Fouche, ed., *The Diary of Adam Tas*, London, Longmans, Green & Co, 1914.

L Guelke & R Shell, op. cit.

J D F Jones, *Storyteller: the many lives of Laurens van der Post*, London, John Murray, 2001.

J E Malherbe, "Jacques Malherbe", *The Huguenot Society of South Africa Bulletin*, 28, 1990-91.

R C Shell, 1994, op. cit.

Image acknowledgements

Images are reproduced with the kind permission of:
The Cape Archives: pp 7, 16, 22, 53, 54, 73, 82, 86, 92, 97, 101, 104, 118, 122
Iziko Museums of Cape Town, Michaelis Collection: pp 58, 61, 83, 98
Museum Africa: cover, pp 11, 15, 21, 25, 28, 30, 33, 106, 121
The National Library of South Africa: pp 26, 35, 36, 39, 42, 45, 49, 57, 63, 67
The Stellenbosch Museum: p 77
The Wellington Museum: pp 18, 19

The images on pp 110, 111 & 113 are taken from *The Huguenots of South Africa 1688-1988* by Pieter Coertzen, Tafelberg, 1988 (with thanks to the Huguenot Society of South Africa). Those on pp 59, 100 & 119 are from *South African History Told in Pictures* by E C Godée-Molsbergen & J V Visscher, S L van Looy, Amsterdam, 1913; on pp 87 & 116 from *Yesterday's Dress* by A A Telford, Purnell, 1972; and on p 89 from *Clothing Fashions in South Africa* by Daphne H. Strutt, A A Balkema, 1975.

The photograph on p 24 is by A P Rose-Innes and those on pp 68, 69, 80 are by H J Rose-Innes.